Contents

Introduction

My Family is a TV sitcom that plays on the generational divide that continually exists – the need for adults and children to have their own 'space' and the right not to always have it invaded by the other. For generations, the church has followed similar principles with a clear division between Adult Worship and Family or All-age Worship – and equally, for generations, adults and children alike have accepted that this is 'the way it is'.

However, the staggering statistics from the 1990s of the haemorrhaging from the church and, in particular, that of the loss of children and young people, has brought the issue into sharp focus. The fact that contemporary childhood is much shorter with the advent of the the Internet and satellite TV, combined with far more modern styles of worship song being available, means that the divide between the generations has shrunk and the need for quality (rather than token) combined worship is even greater.

In the past, churches have often aimed for quantity rather than quality – by putting enormous amounts into services in the hope that there will be something for everyone. The result has often been services that are about survival rather than worship. So how can we do it?

In the other books in this series, years B and C of the *DIY Guide to All-age Worship,* we have looked at the thinking behind All-age Worship as well as some practical advice about how to use resources and people in the most effective way. The introduction to this book seeks to answer some of the Frequently Asked Questions involving All-age Worship in order to try and find a way through the problems that inevitably arise.

Putting on Family or All-age Worship services that can be accessible and relevant to people of whatever age, gender, marital and parental status is an awesome prospect that results in the panic reaction in some churches of doing the same service they do every Sunday, but introducing an element that is aimed at children. Others have a service closely resembling a mini-riot which says little, but very loudly. The question that we are left with is therefore how to give a meaning to All-age Worship, without making it heavy and, by implication, boring. Alternatively, how can we convey a concept in a service without losing the profound nature of the concept itself – in other words how can we avoid accusations of being flippant or being entertaining for the sake of being entertaining. In a nutshell – how can we achieve the balance?

Rewind

In book B in this series, we looked at general principles surrounding All-age Worship and came to the conclusion that it was vital to know the key point you are trying to make in the service and know the answers to three key questions:

- What is the one thing you want people to take away?
- What is the one issue you want to challenge people about?
- What is the one thing you want people to apply in their lives?

I aim most All-age Worship at the 7-year-olds in the congregation and aim to talk in language that they can understand, avoiding jargon wherever possible and explaining things in ways I hope they can appreciate. However, within that language and approach, I aim to provide thoughts that will stimulate discussion and further thought in the adults present. Pitching All-age Worship in this way does not mean banal and thin worship, because the average 7-year-old is able to cope with concepts and a world view far beyond the 7-year-old of previous generations.

The services in this book are based on Year A in the cycle of readings that are contained in *Common Worship* and the service plans themselves are based around the 'Service of the Word', an informal service containing the elements that make up a balanced act of worship:

- A **Clear Beginning**
- A **Prayer of Repentance** (Confession)
- A **Prayer of the Assurance of Forgiveness** (absolution)
- Expressions of **Worship,** spoken or sung
- A **Reading** from the Bible
- Some form of **Teaching**
- **Prayers** including our requests to God (intercession)
- The **Lord's Prayer**
- A **Statement of what we believe**
- An **Ending** that draws together our thoughts

For a detailed analysis of these items, see the *DIY Guide to All-age Worship; Year B* (Published by Kevin Mayhew).

Frequently asked questions _____

Many people acknowledge that in some churches there would need to be a considerable amount of groundwork before the type of All-age Worship service outlined in this book could take place. Practical issues and traditional attitudes might have a bearing, and questions of a more profound nature would need to be addressed. I remember a Bishop saying: 'I love tradition. I love tradition so much I think I'll even start a few of my own!'

The majority of the traditions in our church stem from the people who have been worshipping faithfully in that place for many years. The hardest part of being a member of a church is to see others dismantle or change the work that you have spent years building up – not because what you did was wrong or inappropriate but because it was right for the time when you did it but is not now. For those who now build modern forms of church worship, it is going to be just as hard to see others doing it to us in a couple of decades time - or sooner!

One fundamental problem that All-age Worship has to deal with is that of the relationship with the Eucharist or Holy Communion. For All-age Worship to engage with children and young people, it requires a certain amount of liveliness to be a natural part of the service (though not always, as that would be exhausting!).

The problem comes when it is time to: 'Be quiet because we are going to have Communion now.' This is a perfectly appropriate approach to the solemnity and gravity of the Eucharist – and yet it can have the potential to squash the good work that has been achieved in the earlier part of the service.

My own view is that it is very hard to truly do an 'All-age Communion Service' – as opposed to a 'Communion Service involving all ages'! There is an important difference between the two: the former is a service specifically aimed at being for all ages in its entirety, whereas the latter is only aimed at being all-age in parts. So is it possible to have a true All-age Holy Communion Service? I would say: 'Only in certain circumstances', such as Christmas, Easter or a festival where the underlying nature of the festival allows for such things – and time may not be quite so important.

What are the questions we should be asking?

Probably the most important issue in all types of worship, but especially in All-age Worship is that of 'answering the right question'. Several writers have recently noted that those born before 1950 were of a generation that grew up understanding and accepting the authority of scripture (whether or not they believed it) and so the question asked by that generation was (and still is): 'Is it true?' The response of the church has been to call upon the acknowledged authority of scripture to prove that it is.

The writers have then noted that the baby boomer generation of 1950-1970 ask a different question, relating to the fact that growing up in a world of technology led to the main question in life being: 'Does it work?' In an increasingly pluralistic society and radically changing world, the question of how Christianity related in practical terms to their own needs, the question was a different one, especially when those asking it were trying to see if Christianity could still work in the materialism of the 1980s.

Sadly, the message and worship of many churches was still addressing the questions of the previous generation and, as a result, the fall away of the '80s and '90s grew ever greater.

As we have arrived in the twenty-first century we are facing a generation who are so used to change that it is a natural part of their daily life – in fact, it is a generation who thrive on change and are easily bored without it. That leads earlier generations to say that young people today could learn to be satisfied - but that is simply not the way that they 'are'. They are no longer interested as to whether something is true or if it works – they want to know: 'How does it feel?' There is a desire for authenticity in the life of the church and its worship. The positive side of this has been an amazing response by young people to put the Christian ethos into practical social action – and to see it infiltrate every part of their lives. The flip side is that young people reject Christianity where they see it being lost in Sunday religious observance rather than 24/7 lifestyle.

It could be said that the idealism of teenagers is getting more extreme and that all we are seeing are the evolutionary results of this !

So the reality of worship today is that the question being asked by children and young people is not the one that the church has traditionally answered. 'How does it feel?' cannot be answered with: 'It is true, because the Bible says it is'. For a start, a large percentage of children and young people now grow up without any access to the Bible and regard it much in the way that previous generations regarded the Koran – as some kind of mystical, remote document only understood by its religious adherents. The result is that the Bible has no authority in the eyes of young people – and even many Christian young people do not see the Bible as relevant unless it is lived out in the lives of their parents. Young people seek authenticity – a warts-and-all Christianity that seeks to be real 24/7.

This has to have real effects upon our worship – as someone said to me: 'The church can no longer hide behind liturgy.' Our services cannot be a constant rehashing of the same material. We need to be inventive and seek to worship with integrity. When Jesus said in John 4 that worshippers could worship anywhere but must worship 'in spirit and in truth', there was a thought that applied directly into this situation.

One immediate result is that those speaking can no longer hide behind dogma or simple doctrine, or simply fire Bible verses at their congregations. The services in this book contain scripture at their heart and everything is scripturally based, but each reference to the Bible must have a relevance in itself, rather than a cry for authority.

Equally, dogmatic statements about what Christians should or shouldn't do are no longer appropriate: what we say needs to be based on reality. For example, Christians shouldn't tell lies – but they do! We need to be realistic about what living an authentic Christian life means – maybe we need to revisit Jesus' vision statement of the Kingdom of God in Matthew 5 to 7 in order to get the picture of what he had in mind for us.

In short, for our worship to be relevant to twenty-first-century people of all ages, it needs to have an authenticity and an honesty. If it does, then it will answer the questions: 'Is it true?' and 'Does it work?' as well as the question that this generation asks: 'How does it feel?'

What is a Service of the Word?

When I was young, a menu was something in a posh restaurant and nothing more! To have a choice was amazing – but usually the choice was either the size of the steak or what you had with it! For the Church, particularly the Church of England, the menu was along the lines of the Model T Ford . . . any service you like, so long as it is BCP!

The advent of the *Alternative Service Book* in 1980 began the thought of a more open style of worship and the thought there could be a choice of, for example, Eucharistic prayers, enabling the service leader to select one appropriate to the theme of the service.

Nowadays, menus are everywhere, from the computer screen to the intensely irritating telephone ones – but the problem is that sometimes we don't like having to make a choice and actually prefer to stick with the safety of 'meat and two veg' worship, rather than the exotic menus that might stretch our ecclesiastical taste buds.

The advent of Common Worship has enabled the Church of England to offer an amazing menu of resources to be blended into tasty worship! Under the next section: 'The Services and how to use them', you will find a layout of the service which forms the basis for All-age Worship in the C of E, the Service of the Word. It is a service that allows each component to be tailor-made for the themes you are looking at and to find forms of worship that are accessible to your congregation (and that varies greatly from church to church).

The temptation is to find one set of choices and stick with them, in the same way that the same items are often ticked off on a takeaway food menu! The result is that new traditions form and people complain when you move on from them! There is a risk element in all that surrounds All-age Worship and we must be ready to risk trying new things.

One of the risks is that of involving people who do not have a full understanding of worship – the problem is not in their gifting but in their application. I have regularly been at services where the person leading is very good at the leading 'in theory' but has not been guided into the 'practice' of what the service is trying to achieve in reality. They have chosen their favourite Confession or Creed (or even left one of them out because they didn't think it was necessary) and have ended up with a service that has been unbalanced.

The Service of the Word is a wonderful gift to worship as it gives so many possibilities for both great or awful worship! The job of the church leader is to use it creatively and encourage those who are involved in services to understand how it all works. It should perhaps be mentioned that, for a few churches, the leader is the one who needs to understand how these things work – as a church leader myself, I know only too well of the things it is *assumed* that I already know, when nobody has ever shown me! So be gentle with your leader and work together to get the best out of this service – it is worth it!

I have an ancient church

It is truly amazing that when the Saxons and Normans built all those churches, they didn't make provision for the possibility of an OHP and a screen! But the fact is that they didn't – and for some churches, All-age Worship is hampered by the restrictions of the building in which they meet.

One (highly) radical solution is not to meet in the church and use either the church hall (which may be equally unsuitable) or meet in the local school. This is radical, yes, but has the most amazing potential to transform both the opportunities for worship as well as to create possibilities to invite others into a non-threatening building. The layout of such alternative venues may need some working on and provide challenges of their own but the essential need is for a focal point of the worship which would probably be a table at the front of the hall. This would need to be covered with some kind of white cloth and it is suggested you might bring a cross from church to place on it as a 'connection' with the usual venue. Depending on whether the service involves Communion, other furniture may be needed, too. Also, remember that the acoustics of a hall may be different to those of the church and if a hearing loop is installed in church, those who rely on it will need to be helped in the alternative location.

An alternative location is one possibility but what if it is not the solution due to unavailability of an alternative or unwillingness to move by the congregation? The latter is a matter that needs careful consideration but might be solved by having two services in different places or offers of lifts to the new location. But, for some churches, you are stuck with what you have.

The only answer is to stand back and see the building for its opportunities rather than its challenges – but I speak as one who tries to see the glass as half full rather than half empty! The challenge is to us the *whole* building rather than just the places you might usually use – read from the pulpit, from the back of church . . . or by radio microphone from the vestry. Anywhere but the lectern! Involve the whole congregation in the service – give them 'crowd' lines in readings or get them to move (now there's a challenge!).

Putting up a screen is not always easy in some churches as it might obscure something that is important to some. If you need, for example, to put a screen in such a place that the Lord's Table cannot be seen, put a table in front of the screen with a small cross on it to help those for whom this might be a problem. If the only way to have a screen in church means that an element of the congregation (or the choir) have to move, then some sensitive diplomacy in advance is necessary but can be greatly rewarding in both the effect on worship and also on what can be difficult relationships! The bottom line is to stand back and ask 'how' the service might work. Be creative and adventurous – like the advent of a new dish on the menu, the taste buds will adjust to it!

We have no children in our church

The very title All-age Worship relies on a certain assumption – that people of all ages will be there to worship! For many churches, this is simply not the reality and leads to many other questions, such as: 'Is there a need to keep trying?' and: 'How can we encourage families and children to come along?' This leads to the need for a church to make decisions about resources and the targeting of worship.

Many churches now have a mission statement as to the day-to-day thinking behind what they are doing as a church and/or a vision statement as to what they are aiming to do in the long run. It is important that the approach to All-age Worship is integral to these statements and this thinking not because the children and young people are the church of tomorrow but because they are the church of today – which needs building up. Even if your church has not got an overall mission/vision statement, there is no reason why you cannot work on a vision for your All-age Worship.

The difficulty for many churches in this position is the need to grasp nettles that will, in the short term, hurt and these nettles usually include facing up to those who will grumble about inappropriate worship when there are few children present. But if the nettles are grasped in such a way as to tackle the issues and can be seen as part of a vision, then be brave!

So how can you deal with the problem of not having children at your All-age Worship ? Just a few suggestions . . .

- Link all Baptism and Thanksgiving Services to All-age Worship Sundays. If those are the only times when Baptisms and Thanksgivings are offered, then it will mean that it is more than likely there will be children and young people present along with family and friends of the candidate.

- Link Baptism and Thanksgiving families to another family or couple at church in order to provide a link with someone who will be at church. If you suggest to the families that they might come to all-age services before the Baptism or Thanksgiving, then there will be at least someone they know.

- Build on links with local schools, especially if they have a church foundation. Why not hold the school foundation day service or an end-of-term service on a Sunday? If the building provides a problem (as in the previous section), invite the school to the service you are going to hold *in* the school hall.

- Have a church 'Fun Day' with games and stalls, finishing with a service (if you finish with the service, there is a greater likelihood that people will stay than if you begin with one!)

We have no OHP or data projector

The amount of technology involved in modern education means that schools are bursting with equipment that their forebears could only dream of! If you do not have an OHP, then it is quite possible to pick one up second hand, if you are willing to sacrifice a certain amount of quality. If you can raise sufficient money to buy a new one, along with a screen, then it is certainly worth the money. However, many schools (especially those with Church Foundation or connections) are willing to be generous with their resources and will consider lending it to you.

There are two keys to borrowing such equipment – one is a sufficiently good relationship with the school to enable you to feel able to ask and the other is having someone sufficiently capable of using the technology. It is fairly obvious that it is embarrassing (in the extreme) if you come to church with the technology, but with no one capable of making it work! However, making technology work is often a case of trial and error and so a dry run is always suggested (to check, for example, that all the leads are working) and it is always a good idea to have a spare bulb and a spare set of acetates of the songs or the song numbers available for when the projector decides it doesn't want to work!

If you have someone who can set up the technology at home, preferably on their own laptop, then approaching the school can be done with confidence. It is also worth checking the insurance situation on equipment which is borrowed in order that you are covered against any breakages or theft. And, in saying that, it is not a good idea to leave the projector all set up in church with the church open and unattended!

Which is better – books, service sheets or an OHP?

'Knowing your limits' is a good maxim to apply to All-age Worship in general terms. Knowing what you can genuinely achieve in terms of putting on a service involves an awareness of the congregation and their needs. Putting on a three-act drama involving 25 people for a congregation of 15 is not necessarily viable! Knowing your congregation is vital and so you need to think about the appropriate use of an OHP or projector.

The advantages of an OHP are that people do not need to have any books for the service and that all the liturgy and songs are able to be read by everyone without the need for them to search through several books! That is often the case with All-age Worship, as resources may come from several different books – and can severely limit what you can reasonably use. Another advantage of an OHP is that the singing in the service may be better because people are looking up rather than having their noses in a book. This can sometimes be a contentious matter as some people like to have a book to hang on to !

The disadvantages of an OHP are that you are reliant on technology and the potential for a bulb to blow at a crucial moment. Admittedly this is a rarity, but ALL technology can misbehave! Using books or service sheets can mean losing a degree of flexibility, as you are then limited to what is on the sheet.

Either way, preparation is needed and whoever does it needs to have access to a computer in order to prepare either the service sheet or acetates, ensuring that the text is readable. It is also worth noting that there may well be those who are old or infirm and cannot stay standing for any length of time – and any use of a screen is limited for them. Separate song sheets (or large print copies for those with impaired sight) are always a good idea – but beware of offering these to those who do not want to use the screen as a matter of principle!

All options have their limitations – the key is to find what works for you and your congregation!

We don't have people with the right gifts

One of the advantages of All-age Worship is that those who usually lead the children in Sunday school are able to come into church that week – or at least that is the theory! Some will see it as an opportunity for a well-earned rest – with a considerable amount of justification. For others, to be landed upon to 'do' the All-age Worship is not what they want and they are reluctant to join the team. Equally, those who are teachers for a living are often reluctant to also be teachers on a Sunday.

The result of this is that the All-age Worship can often fall onto the shoulders of those who, at first sight, are least qualified or gifted to do it, particularly if the vicar or church leader is wonderful at preaching long sermons but not gifted in this particular area (and that may be putting it politely!). My own experience is that those who I have listed above are often scared of doing things because of the fear of being roped into doing it every month – especially if it becomes clear that they are good at it! So one suggestion is that you negotiate with people as to how often you would expect them to take part in the services and, most of all, stick to the agreement. Most will be willing to take part on a termly basis, say three times a year, and will do so with great enthusiasm.

Another thought is to see if there are those in churches around you who are willing to help out in this area of church life. This can be a highly effective way of linking churches and growing the relationships – especially if you discover that you, as a church, have people who are gifted in areas that the other church is lacking.

A final thought is to be bold in looking for people who might have a previously undiscovered talent. They may need a little (or a lot of) encouragement and I would suggest that to use new talent in every service is a risky strategy unless you are certain of the confidence and gifts of those involved, but an occasional brave step may be worth it in the long run.

Where do I get resources such as music, graphics or clipart?

Vast amounts of resources are becoming available and often, like the Common Worship menu mentioned earlier, there is a temptation to stick with what you already have. The result of this is that you find yourself singing the same songs and using the same clipart year after year! Being aware of the resources that are available to you is important – but it's equally important to find out what works for you. Some resources and ideas work brilliantly in one church but not in another. Equally, some churches may tell you of something that did not work in their context, but will work beautifully in your own situation.

Many books offer 'off-the-shelf' services to make life easier, but there are also many ideas books available offering thoughts that could be of use to your situation or services. Ultimately, those putting on the services must have a high degree of 'ownership' of what they do and the more they own it the better.

In the same way, there are enormous music resources available and, being realistic, some are considerably better and more usable than others. Finding what is appropriate to you, again, is a matter of experimentation and trial and error, but if you invite those involved to take the resources away and explore them for themselves, the potential usage is high. You could buy a series of worship tapes or CDs and pass them round members of the music group to listen to in the car and then to discuss which could be learned in church.

It is also a good idea, if you have anyone who visits Christian festivals such as New Wine or Spring Harvest, to send them off with a budget to buy copies of anything they come across that they believe would be relevant to your church needs. It is also worth using the bookstalls at these festivals as an opportunity to look at clipart and graphic packages to see which is most appropriate to you. Another regular event is the Christian Resources Exhibition, where free samples of many resources are offered to visitors. This takes place regionally.

Another idea is to make good use of the Internet. A vast warehouse of resources is building up and, as with all that has been mentioned so far, it is a case of being 'good in parts'. There are some excellent resources on the Internet but finding them sometimes requires dedication to the task.

Ultimately, finding out what works for you requires you to look and learn from others. Imitation is the sincerest form of flattery but it is also a great way of getting some good things in your church!

The services and how to use them _____

The following 12 services have been designed to offer as much flexibility as possible and will enable people to fit things into the way their services already run – or to build complete services around them using the 'Service of the Word' already mentioned. This is loosely based around Year A of the Common Worship Lectionary but may also be applied to readings from other years.

In some cases, the tradition of the church means that it will involve a Holy Communion service and although, as has been said, this is not always recommended, this will not be a problem, as the elements contained in the service work as well in a Eucharistic setting as in a non-Eucharistic setting. It should also be noted that the ideas that follow are just that – ideas that can be adapted or changed to fit the setting, the congregation or the nature of the service. The songs suggested for the services may work with some churches better than others: every church has the songs which are known and loved, but it is important that new songs are introduced which apply to new generations of worshippers.

Ultimately, the services must be owned by those who lead and speak at them and that is why there is a large element of generality about some of the items. Each service is a unique act of worship that must express the emotions, the thanks and praise, the needs and hurts, and the hearts' desires of those present. Each service is an offering to the congregation and to God and therefore needs time and prayer in preparation.

Each service has a title – and a reading. This may be helpful as a name tag for the service and used on posters and publicity.

The three questions that were asked earlier then follow: with an answer based on the thinking of the person who prepared the material. If you choose to amend this service to your own plans and needs, then these questions still need to be answered – and the answers might be different!

A short introduction follows that tries to explain the thinking behind the service and how it might fit into the church's year.

Preparing the church
The twenty-first century is characterised by a generation that is far more visually-based in its learning than previous generations. Moving the church around or displaying pictures relating to ideas in the service to follow can, therefore, be a great help in the conveying of concepts. At the same time, there are other preparations that often need to be thought about in advance and these are also mentioned under this heading.

Beginning
All services need a beginning and this may be just one suggestion. The important thing is that the leader is himself or herself and that any welcome is not forced. Equally, avoid any habitual greeting that might be amusing once or twice but can be cringingly embarrassing for those who have seen or heard it several dozen times before!

Songs
Some songs that may be suitable for the theme of the service are suggested. Each church has its own set of song books and the songs suggested in this book are

available in either *The Source* (Kevin Mayhew), *Mission Praise* (Marshall Pickering) or *Songs of Fellowship* (Kingsway Music).

A Short Talk and Teaching
There are a wide variety of options available to those organising an all-age service – be adventurous but keep to the point, be creative but know what you are doing – and most of all, enjoy yourself and challenge yourself.

A Prayer of Repentance and Statement of What We Believe
Suggestions as to which element of A Prayer of Repentance and Statement of What We Believe are used (both from *Common Worship*) follow, possibly with some idea of how they might be explained to those present.

Intercessions and Lord's Prayer
Some suggestions as to how the Intercessions might be structured are also added, as well as a reminder regarding the inclusion of the Lord's Prayer.

Reading from the Bible
A Reading from the Bible is suggested - usually a Gospel reading, and usually one from the Common Worship Year A Lectionary readings - other readings may be added as necessary.

An Ending
As with the beginning, a good and effective ending is vital and some suggestions are made (with the assumption that some form of prayer of Blessing will also be used).

Advent

The ultimate party – Romans 13:11-14; Luke 14:15-23

- **What is the one thing you want them to take away?**
- ✓ That Heaven is a party nobody should miss!
- **What is the one issue you want to challenge them about?**
- ✓ Do other things matter more than God?
- **What is the one thing you want them to apply in their lives?**
- ✓ To be excited about life now – because of what is to come.

Advent is not an easy subject for All-age Worship because many of the images and stories Jesus used about Judgement and Hell are really quite scary! This service uses the second reading for Advent Sunday together with a changed Gospel reading in order to emphasise the positive aspects of Advent – that Jesus is coming back to bring his followers for a party that will never end!

Preparing the church

Prepare the church as though a party is about to take place – balloons, streamers, party banners (not with Happy Birthday on, though!) . . . anything that brings a feeling of being at a party. You could have fairy cakes or party-type food included in the refreshments after the service. If you have an OHP available, put up the slide which says 'Invitation to a party' **(OHP 1)** or, if you have access to a digital projector, put up a series of slides which are invitations to the 'Party to end all parties' .

Beginning

Welcome everyone by asking what time they woke up this morning! Ask what was the first thought they had (was it: 'Oh no! It's Sunday, and that means church!') Do not take too long about this – it is only to introduce the thought about anticipation.

Reading from the Bible

Read Romans 13:11-14 from *The Message* – preferably using a reader with an excited voice – leading into the first song or hymn . . .

Songs

Advent hymns such as 'Come thou long-expected Jesus' or 'Lo, he comes with clouds descending' are traditional hymns that might be used, although 'At the name of Jesus' might be more accessible. Songs such as 'Soon and very soon' or 'Joy to the world' are highly appropriate – as is the simple (but profound) chorus 'Heaven is a wonderful place.'

Prayer of repentance

The Confession at the top of page 125 in *Common Worship* and the Absolution at the top of page 137 are suitable.

Reading from the Bible

Read Luke 14:15-23 from a modern translation, leading into a sketch . . .

Sketch

The Parable of the Great Banquet is a story Jesus told whilst out for a meal with a Pharisee. It was a very pointed story that tried to get his host to see that he was the one missing out. Missing out on the party is a fear of most of us – not being deemed uncool or unpopular is a driving force behind most of the advertising that is put before us day by day. But the message of this parable (and this sketch) is that being cool on the outside is different to being cool on the inside!

How you might use this sketch

The only props needed are a table with a phone, but if the church is decorated with streamers and balloons, so much the better. The opening invitation slide **(OHP 1)** helps to set the scene. The narrator is to one side of the 'stage', next to the phone – if it can be made to ring, so much the better, but if not, someone off-stage imitating a phone would add to proceedings! The narrator should be in a suit and shades and should be a showman – either over-the-top extrovert, or deeply cool, in delivery. Characters A and E are in the middle of the stage, dressed as uncool as possible. Be careful to either overdo it in a way that is a ridiculous caricature rather than embarrass those present who may actually not be that cool in the eyes of their peers. Characters B, C and D are to the other side of the stage, and are dressed in cool clothes, maybe with mobiles to their ears. Club music (preferably with no voices) is playing. You may need to offer contemporary party examples instead of the ones mentioned in the first few lines . . .

Narrator	Laydieees and Gen-tle-men!!! This is it! This is the one!
	You have heard about the Posh 'n' Becks party!
	You've seen the pictures in *Hello* of the legendary post-gig parties of the Rolling Stones!
	You have read the reports of the Hollywood parties of the rich and famous!
	But nothing, NOTHING, compares to this . . . the biggest . . . the best . . .
	The party of all time!
	The party that goes *beyond* time!
	The party . . .
	(A takes a step forward)

A	Excuse me!
Narrator	WHAT?
A	Can I come?
Narrator	No – you're not invited … go away!
	(A takes a step back)
	Now, where was I? Oh yes, the party.
	The invitations have been sent out!
	The party is ON!
	It is TIME to PARTTTTYYYY!
	(A takes a step forward)
A	Excuse me!
Narrator	WHAT?
A	Why can't I come?
Narrator	Have you got an invitation?
A	Not at the moment
Narrator	Then can you come?
A	I suppose not.
Narrator	Then go away and stop irritating me.
	(A takes a step back. The phone rings)
	Hello … yes … fine … OK … I'm on my way.
	Right, it's time to party – let's go and get the guests.
	(Narrator moves over to B, C and D)
Narrator	Hi guys! It is time!
B	What?
Narrator	It's time!
C	For what?
Narrator	For *the* party!
D	*What* party?
Narrator	WHAT PARTY?
	The party … The *only* party … The party to end all parties!
	Come on … it's happening … right now!
B	No – don't want to.
Narrator	Why ever not?
B	Because … I've got a new flat and it needs decorating.
Narrator	*(Total disbelief)* You WHAT?
	You would rather spend the day up to your armpits in wallpaper paste than go to the ultimate party?
B	It's my flat and I'll paint it if I want to.
Narrator	*(To C)* Boorrring! What about you? You coming to the party?
C	No … I've got my new car outside … I'm going for a drive.
Narrator	*(Disbelief)* Car … drive … rather than the ultimate party?
C	That's right.
Narrator	*(Shakes head)* Sad … very sad.
	(Turns to D) Don't tell me …
	… you've got homework?
	… you've got to wash your hair?
	… you've …
D	No, I'd rather be with my mates.

Narrator	You'd rather be with your mates?
D	Yeah, if they're not going, neither am I.
Narrator	But the invitation was to you, as an individual.
D	Nah, not interested.
	(B, C and D all turn back to each other and start talking)
Narrator	*(Goes to phone, picks it up and dials a few numbers)*
	Um . . . . Heaven, we've got a problem! They don't want to come.
	(Pause, as narrator listens. His eyes get bigger as he is given further instructions)
	No . . . you cannot be serious . . . no . . . surely not . . .
	(He looks at A and E)
	Them!!!!???
	OK, if you say so . . . yes, you do say so.
	(Mumbles) It seems you're invited.
A	Sorry, did you say something?
Narrator	It seems you're invited.
E	Us?
Narrator	Yes . . . you. It seems the party is now open to everyone.
A	You know something?
Narrator	What?
E	We may appear uncool on the outside, but on the inside . . .
A and E	We're as cool as anything!
	(A and D break into a cool dance, or pose – or something indicating coolness!)
Narrator	*(Brightens up)* Come on, then . . . we've got a party to go to.
	(Narrator, A and E begin to walk off. Narrator turns back)
Narrator	It doesn't matter how cool or uncool you think you may be, the invitation to the party to end all parties is open to everyone . . . absolutely everyone.
	There can always be a reason to say 'no':
	things can always get in the way or we might feel we are not cool enough.
	But the invitation is open to everyone, *absolutely* everyone.
	Turning down the invitation is a risk, just as much as accepting the invitation.
	God invites you, you, you, you . . . and me, to the party.
	What about you, do you want to come?
	(He turns and walks off)

Teaching

Little teaching is needed as the sketch aims to provide most of the challenge of the reading. A short talk, drawing together the following thoughts, is all that is required . . .

- Jesus told people that heaven is a wonderful place, like a never-ending party.
- Jesus said that everyone was invited – but not everyone would want to go.
- Jesus made it possible for us to go to the party when he died and rose again.
- When Jesus went back to be with his Father in heaven (the Ascension), he promised to come back one day to take those who wanted to be with him to do just that – to be with him!
- Jesus will come back one day – he promised to do so, and he keeps his promises.
- No one knows when that will be.
- You want to be at that party – and you hope and pray that everyone else does!

Statement of what we believe

Use the Affirmation of Faith number 6 on page 148 of *Common Worship* – it may need a little explanation, but say that it talks about the promise that one day Jesus will return.

Intercessions and Lord's Prayer

Give thanks to God for the promise that Jesus will return and ask that all Christians may live with a real excitement of the thought of being at God's party in heaven for ever. Pray that others will see the excitement and want to come to the party for themselves.

Ending

As a final prayer, remind everyone that they are invited to the party to end all parties and that you hope and pray that they will want to be there. If you have party food available, invite everyone to start the party now!

It's **PARTY TIME!**

You are invited to . . .

. . . the party to end all PARTIES

Who wants to be a Christmas Clever Clogs? – John 1:1-14

- **What is the one thing you want them to take away?**
- ✓ That there is a point to all that you do at Christmas.
- **What is the one issue you want to challenge them about?**
- ✓ Do *you* understand why Jesus came?
- **What is the one thing you want them to apply in their lives?**
- ✓ To see that Christmas has effects all year.

How often do you hear people muttering in the queue at the supermarket 'Why do we do it?' as their trolley laden with food, drink, presents and goodies approaches the checkout! It is a very common question and one that requires a degree of searching in order to find the answer. Based on the TV show *Who Wants To Be a Millionaire?*, this service relies on a small degree of preparation and a large degree of audience participation – which should not be hard to find! You will need to find an extrovert host, a contestant primed to 'volunteer' and a 'friend' with a mobile phone. If (like the author), you live in an area where mobile signals are weak, you may need to revise this part of the service!

Preparing the church

If you have an OHP available, prepare slides of the show title and the questions – and have the title slide up before the service. Have the prizes 'on display' on a table at the front of church. If you have access to a digital projector, find (or take) pictures of the prizes and use them as a rolling display. If possible, have a contestant's swivel chair at the front of church.

Beginning

A simple welcome to the service with an introduction to the first hymn is all that is needed!

Songs

'Once in royal David's city' would be good to begin the service as it tells something of the background to the Christmas story. Include carols such as 'Away in a manger' or 'Come and join the celebration' that the youngest will be able to join in with, especially as the latter is used in schools. 'O come, all ye faithful' or 'Hark, the herald-angels sing' are the usual choices to finish the service.

Short talk

Ask some traditional Christmas morning questions . . . Who has opened a present already today? Who hasn't? Awake earliest? Who woke up their parents?
Get children (and the adults) to show the presents they have brought to church. Does anyone know *why* they were given the present they were? Did they really need it? Ask if anyone knows why we give and receive presents at Christmas – and use it as an introduction to the Confession.

Prayer of Repentance

The Christmas Confession on page 123 of *Common Worship* and the second Absolution on page 135 are suitable.

Reading from the Bible

Read John 1:1-14 using a modern translation, or paraphrase the story in *The Message* or the New Living Bible. It is not an easy lesson for children to understand so try and use a good, well-prepared reader.

Teaching

The teaching takes the form of a game show called 'Who wants to be a Christmas Clever Clogs?' If someone else is to do this, suggest that they run up to the front of the stage immediately after the previous part of the service has finished, while the 'title' slide is put up **(OHP 2)**, and they can ask the audience (as a game show host) . . . 'Who wants to be a Christmas Clever Clogs?' They may need to ask it a couple of times to get people switched on to what is happening – and then they need to ask for a 'volunteer' contestant – and the prearranged member of the congregation should hopefully respond!

Having got the contestant in the chair (see 'Preparing the church'), the host finds out who they are, what they do and what family they have – even if everyone knows all this already! Tell them that there are some fantastic prizes to be won in the service this morning, including . . .

- Packet of raisins
- Piece of tinsel
- Satsuma
- Cracker
- Chocolate money
- Christmas pud
- Box of chocolates

Remind them that they have three lifelines:
- Ask the audience
- Phone a friend
- 50/50

So they are only 'Seven questions away from ONE box of Chocolates'
Right – let's play: 'Who wants to be a Christmas Clever Clogs?'

You need some help from the audience at this point – they need to provide the music that goes along the lines of 'diddly-diddly-diddly-diddly-dee' (You need to see the TV show to understand this! You might like to get people to have their arms raised and to gradually lower them (at the same time as doing the music and wiggling their fingers!)

Begin the quiz, with frequent catchphrases such as 'Are you sure?' or 'Is that your final answer?' or 'You've won a .... – but we don't want to give you just that'.

Question 1 for a packet of raisins:
Who was Jesus' mother?
a) Myrtle, b) Mabel, c) Mary, d) Madge

Question 2 for a piece of tinsel:
What did a Wise Man bring to give to Jesus?
a) Frankincense, b) Frank Butcher, c) Frank Skinner, d) Frank Spencer

Question 3 for a satsuma:
Which of these animals is not usually present in a Christmas Nativity scene?
a) Donkey, b) Sheep, c) Cow, d) Three-toed sloth

Question 4 for a cracker:
Which of these books tells the story of Christmas?
a) Matthew, b) John, c) Psalms, d) Revelation

Question 5 for the chocolate money:
When Isaiah predicted Jesus' birth which of these descriptions did he NOT use?
a) Prince of Peace, b) Everlasting King, c) Mighty God, d) Wonderful Counsellor

The answer is Everlasting King – Isaiah calls him the 'Everlasting Father'. You may like to suggest the contestant asks the audience and/or uses 50/50 at this point! You may like to help proceedings by 'highlighting' the correct answer!

Question 6 for a Christmas pudding:
How many words in total are there in the seven readings in a carol service?
a) 1656, b) 1456, c) 1856, d) 2056 – (The answer is 1656, given in the NIV)

They will obviously not have a clue – use the 'phone a friend' lifeline by having a mobile phone ready and say you have a friend who knows the answer – they will be in the congregation with their mobile switched on, ready to give the answer.

Build up the tension to the final question by saying they can walk away with the Christmas pudding or go for the big one (a box of chocolates) – but they can look at the final question and still walk away.

Who wants to be a . . . CHRISTMAS Clever Clogs?

You're just 7 questions away from a **whole** box of chocolates!

Is that your final answer?

Question 7 for a box of chocolates

Why was Jesus born?

a) To be a good man, b) To be a good teacher, c) To be nice to people, d) To grow up and save the world from sin.

The contestant will hopefully know the right answer! Congratulate them and present them with the box of chocolates and a big round of applause.

Make the point that Chris Tarrant often says – The answer is only easy if you know it. So, if you ask many people: 'Do you know the point of Christmas?', it's a good question but the answer is only easy if you know it.

If you don't know the answer you can always go away with the Christmas you already have: a big lunch, *Titanic* on the TV and lots of cards to be recycled – but you haven't got the full value of Christmas.

Some will ask the audience – they will ask other people in the hope that they might get the right answer. But other people can be wrong.
Some might go 50/50 and hope that one of the answers is right.
Some will phone a friend and may or may not get the right answer.

The answer to the question: 'Do you know the point of Christmas?' is a simple one: To grow up and save the world from sin. It's easy if you know the answer – Did you know it?

Put up the last slide with the words: 'When people ask what Christmas is about, the answer is very simple – it is about a baby who was born to grow up and save the world. It is as simple as that.'

Statement of what we believe

Use the Affirmation of Faith number 1 on page 144 of *Common Worship,* saying that it talks about why Jesus came.

Intercessions and Lord's Prayer

Give thanks for all of the aspects of Christmas that make it so exciting – but thank God especially for the reason why Jesus came to earth. Pray for those places where Jesus needs to be: for places where there is war and hatred, places where people are divided, places where people are ill or hurting and in people's hearts, and pray that Jesus will be very real in these places on Christmas Day and all the days ahead.

Ending

As a final prayer, remind people of the reason why Jesus came and pray that amidst all the enjoyment of the rest of the day, they will know the joy that comes from knowing not just that it is Christmas, but *why* it is Christmas.

Question 1
For a packet of raisins

Who was Jesus' mother?

a) Myrtle	b) Mabel
c) Mary	d) Madge

50/50

Ask the audience

Fifty-fifty

Phone a friend

Question 2
For a piece of tinsel

What did a Wise Man bring to give to Jesus?

a) Frankincense	b) Frank Butcher
c) Frank Skinner	d) Frank Spencer

50/50

Ask the audience

Fifty-fifty

Phone a friend

Question 3
For a satsuma

Which of these animals is not usually present in a Christmas Nativity scene?

a) Donkey

b) Sheep

c) Cow

d) Three-toed sloth

Ask the audience

50/50

Fifty-fifty

Phone a friend

Question 4
For a cracker

Which of these books tells the story of Christmas?

a) Matthew

b) John

c) Psalms

d) Revelation

Ask the audience

50/50

Fifty-fifty

Phone a friend

Question 5

For the chocolate money

When Isaiah predicted Jesus' birth which of these descriptions did he NOT use?

a) Prince of Peace

b) Everlasting King

c) Mighty God

d) Wonderful Counsellor

50/50

Ask the audience

Fifty-fifty

Phone a friend

Question 6

For a chocolate pudding

How many words in total are there in the seven readings in a carol service?

a) 1656

b) 1456

c) 1856

d) 2056

50/50

Ask the audience

Fifty-fifty

Phone a friend

Question 7

For a box of chocolates

Why was Jesus born?

a) To be a good man	b) To be a good teacher
c) To be nice to people	d) To grow up and save the world from sin

Ask the audience

Fifty-fifty

Phone a friend

When people ask

(For whatever reason)

What is Christmas all about?

The answer is very simple:	It is about a baby
who was born to grow up	and save the world

It is as simple as that

Epiphany

What do you see? – Matthew 2:1-12

- **What is the one thing you want them to take away?**
- ✓ We all see the same Jesus – but sometimes differently!

- **What is the one issue you want to challenge them about?**
- ✓ What do you *really* see when you think about Christmas?

- **What is the one thing you want them to apply in their lives?**
- ✓ We need to think about what we see.

The point of an optical illusion is that we often see two or more things at the same time – and we are not sure which is the 'correct' image. As we leave Christmas for a new year, the question is often about our perspective on the meaning of what we have just experienced. The importance of the story of the Wise Men was that they saw the real picture immediately.

Preparing the church

If you have an OHP, you might like to use the 'What Do You See?' illusions as acetates **(OHP 3).** Alternatively, you might like to enlarge them and place them around the church for people to look at as they take their seats. If you have a digital projector and access to the Internet, there are several web sites which have 'moving' optical illusions which could be used as a display, both before and during the service.

Beginning

Welcome everyone and ask if their eyes have gone funny yet! Say that even though thinking about Jesus might sometimes be confusing, you hope, as you hear the story of the Wise Men, everyone will, like them, see the real Jesus.

Songs

Following the theme of 'seeing', 'As with gladness, men of old' and 'Angel voices, ever singing', may be appropriate traditional hymns; modern songs such as 'Light of the world' , 'Be still for the presence of the Lord' or 'Shine, Jesus, shine' could be used.

Short talk

Display or draw people's attention to some of the optical illusions and ask everyone what they see. Allow for the possibility that some may find these things easier than others! Ask why these illusions are clever – and offer the answer that they persuade us to see two things at the same time, but we are not sure which is the 'right' picture. Draw attention to the Epiphany theme that Jesus was the light of the whole world, who had come into the world to help us see what was right and wrong and to pay our penalty for the times when we choose the wrong thing.

Prayer of Repentance

Use the *Common Worship* Confession for Resurrection, etc., on page 125 with an explanation that often we do wrong things because we take our eyes off Jesus. The first absolution on page 137 is appropriate, too.

Reading from the Bible

Using a modern translation, read Matthew 2:1-12. This story could easily be dramatised, with some of the readers moving around the church. Some nativity costumes may still be available!

Teaching

Think of all of the main characters in the Christmas story and ask the question: 'What did they see when they saw Jesus?'

- Mary and Joseph .... A child to be looked after, a child who would grow up to save the world (See Luke 1:31-32)
- The shepherds .... A sign that the Saviour had come (See Luke 2:12)
- People in the pub ...... Absolutely nothing! They heard a crying baby!
- Herod .... A challenge (See Matthew 1:1-2)
- Herod's advisers .... The possible fulfilment of a prophecy (See Matthew 1:5-6)

So what about the Wise Men – what did *they* see? Ask what people think that they saw. What they gave as presents suggests what they saw (see Matthew 1:11) . . .

- Gold – for a king: they saw someone who was going to rule the world.
- Frankincense – for a Priest: they saw someone who was going to show people God and help them to relate to him. You may want to explain that frankincense was something that was used in worship.
- Myrrh – for death: they saw someone who was born to die, and to die for a reason. You may want to explain that myrrh was one of the spices that they used to anoint the bodies of people who had died and that they used such things when Jesus died.

The Wise Men saw a king, a priest – and someone who would die for a reason. The question for us is: 'What do we see when we see Jesus?' Some people see Jesus as a revolutionary, some see him as a man dying on a cross for them, some see him as a figure in classical paintings, and some see him as alive and full of life. The truth is that Jesus is all of these things and far more!

Like the optical illusions you began with, Jesus can be seen in many different ways – the important thing for us is that we look hard to see all the different things about Jesus, not to think that we know everything about him.

Statement of what we believe

Use the Affirmation of Faith 5 on page 147 of *Common Worship*, saying that it shows just some of the things we believe about Jesus.

Intercessions and Lord's Prayer

Remembering that Epiphany is about the revelation of Jesus, which was for the whole world, pray that the whole world would see Jesus, in whatever way they might do so. Pray for those places where different views of Jesus may have caused people to disagree, and pray for reconciliation. Above all, pray that the world would see Jesus as its Saviour. Pray for those who are ill or sad, asking that they might be able to see Jesus as someone to help them through their difficult times.

Ending

Ask everyone to think about what they have seen and to keep looking to find new ways to understand him.

What do you see?

⬆ Straight or bent lines?　　　⬇ Duck or rabbit?

⬅ The word Liar or a face?

⬆ Faces or vases?

⬆ How many faces?

First Sunday in Lent

Playing by the rules –
Matthew 4:1-11

- **What is the one thing you want them to take away?**
- ✓ Jesus played by God's rules.

- **What is the one issue you want to challenge them about?**
- ✓ How far are we willing to play by God's rules?

- **What is the one thing you want them to apply in their lives?**
- ✓ To apply God's rules in our lives.

When Jesus sat in the wilderness, thinking and praying about the mission his father had for him, he did not have the Gospels or Paul's letters to meditate upon! His Bible was the Old Testament and his 'rule book' was the Torah, the Law of Moses. Later, when he was challenged about its relevance, he said: 'Do not think that I have come to abolish the Law or the Prophets; I have not come to abolish them but to fulfil them' Matthew 5:17. The idea of laws and rules challenges a post-modern world that lives by feeling and a lack of absolutes – so where do the Ten Commandments fit into this? The idea of this service is that sport relies on rules in order to function properly and that the 'ethos' of any sport relies on an understanding of the 'spirit of the game'. The analogy used here is football, but, with a little thought, this could be applied to any sport.

Preparing the church

Use the OHP to give a title for the service and put items and pictures relating to football around the church. If you have a television and video and can get hold of some football action from 'Match of the Day' show it before the service, using, if possible, film of controversial issues such as fouls or disputed goals. Turn it off when the service begins, as it could easily be a distraction!

Beginning

This needs to be done in a slightly headteacherish tone, with a certain degree of tongue in cheek (!) ... Welcome everyone and say that you hope everyone will enjoy the service but that you need everyone to behave themselves properly and you will be introducing some rules later in the service to ensure that things run smoothly.
(This may be something that needs to be handled sensitively in some churches where, for example, the behaviour of the children in All-age Worship is a cause of 'discussion' among some members of the congregation – it could, equally, be an opportunity to raise the issue!)

Songs

There aren't many songs about discipline or rules, so the themes in the service involve the thought of doing things God's way. 'Shine, Jesus, shine', 'Purify my heart' and 'Seek ye first' have words that reflect this but they may need an introduction to aid understanding. 'We want to see Jesus lifted high' and 'Blessed be the name of the Lord' are appropriate for child-friendly songs, but 'Christ is made the sure foundation' is a rousing hymn that may help to finish the service on the right note!

Short talk

Say that you want some order and discipline in the service and then make up silly rules - e.g. every time the word 'pigeon' is mentioned, everyone stands up, turns round and sits down again - those who don't have to come and stand at the front. Mention pigeon a few times in the next part of the talk and eventually end up with three people at the front who are needed for some part of the service (e.g. to take the collection or make coffee) ... Put up 'You Must Obey The Rules' **(OHP 4)**.

Ask who likes playing sport, especially football, and find out where they play, who they play with and whether they play in a league or just for fun. The point you are trying to make is that whatever level you play at, you need to have some form of rules in order to enjoy the game. E.g. if you play in the park, you still need to know where the goal is and where the sidelines are.

Ask questions about the rules of the game and whether those playing have any special rules for where they play. Ask who decides the rules and who enforces them - so is it by agreement or does someone tell you? Ask if any rules ever change (careful, or you might end up discussing the intricacies of the offside rule!).

Ask what God's rules are and put up the slide which shows which ones Jesus said were the most important ... **(OHP 5)** 'Love the Lord your God with all your heart and with all your soul and with all your strength and with all your mind'; and, 'Love your neighbour as yourself.' Luke 10:27

Ask whether we always play by God's rules and lead into ...

Prayer of Repentance

Say that we are often tempted to cheat in the way we live - to do things our way and disobey God's rules. The General Confession on page 128 of *Common Worship* with the fourth Absolution on page 136 are ideal.

Reading from the Bible

Read Matthew 4:1-11 from a modern translation. The acetate **(OHP 6)** could help to reinforce the story, but having three readers for Jesus, the devil and a narrator would also help.

Teaching

Remind everyone which rules in life Jesus said were the most important **(OHP 5)** and ask from where Jesus learnt his rules. Say that the Old Testament was Jesus' Bible and he used it in the same way as we use the whole Bible.

Ask what rules he had and see how many of the Ten Commandments people can name. Say that these days people sometimes think that these should be called the 'Ten Suggestions' or that there is an eleventh Commandment – 'Thou shalt not get found out' – but they are still important. Put up **OHP 7,** saying that this is perhaps how they would be written today.

Now remember how the devil tempted Jesus and show that he wanted Jesus to play by *his* rules and not God's. Each time Jesus replied with some teaching from his Bible, the Old Testament, to say 'no' to the devil. Ask which of the Ten Commandments the devil tried to persuade Jesus to break – certainly half of them (numbers 1, 2, 8, 9, 10)!

Finally, remind everyone that just as we get on best playing football (or any sport) when we play by the rules which have been laid down by those who know how the game should be played, so we get on best in life if we obey the rules that God has laid down.

Say that you are now in Lent, which is a time when people realise that they need to play by God's rules and that it is a time when we come towards Easter to remember that we need to be forgiven because of the fact that we have not kept the rules.

Statement of what we believe

Creed number 4 on page 147 of *Common Worship* is appropriate in that it describes the way that Jesus dealt with the problem – and how he received the prize by playing by God's rules!

Intercessions and Lord's Prayer

Use the prayers to remind everyone that God's rules are often ignored – it would be good to go through the list and use it as the basis of prayer, but beware of having long prayers because there are so many commandments!

Ending

Remind everyone that playing by the rules is important, not just for ourselves but for people around us, and so it might be a good idea to involve an aspect to the final prayer that invites everyone to recommit themselves to doing things God's way.

*Jesus said the most important
things in life
are to . . .*

'Love the Lord your God
with all your heart
and with all your soul
and with all your strength
and with all your mind'

and

'Love your
neighbour
as yourself'

Luke 10:27

Jesus is tempted . . .

'Tell these stones to
    become bread . . .'

'Throw yourself down . . .
    . . . you will not strike
        your foot against a stone.'

'All this I will give you . . .
    if you will bow down
        and worship me.'

The Ten Commandments for today

1 I am the one and only God.

2 Don't make gods out of pop stars or footballers or anyone else – you only need one God and that's me.

3 Don't use my name without realising how special it is.

4 Make sure you take one day out every week to rest and think about me.

5 Remember what your parents have done for you and show them the respect they deserve.

6 Do not murder people (either in your mind or for real).

7 Keep your relationships true – don't take another person's partner.

8 Don't take what isn't yours.

9 Don't tell lies (little fibs or big whoppers).

10 Don't live life wanting things you haven't got – be satisfied.

Good Friday

He suffered for me –
John 19:16-30,38-42

- **What is the one thing you want them to take away?**
- ✓ What must it have been like to be there on Good Friday?
- **What is the one issue you want to challenge them about?**
- ✓ That we sometimes take what Jesus did for us too lightly.
- **What is the one thing you want them to apply in their lives?**
- ✓ We can live knowing that Jesus died on a cross for *us*.

A short all-age service on Good Friday is often a prelude to a walk of witness and this service is intended to be just that – short and to the point, in the knowledge that a quieter service may take place later in the day. There is sometimes a thought that the violence and suffering of Good Friday is too hard for children to bear, and so we avoid the subject in All-age Worship – but children are far more aware of suffering than their forebears, through the graphic images that news programmes now portray. This does not mean that a graphic 18-certificate portrayal of the cross is in order, only that we should not shy away from the subject. 'He suffered for me' is a simple and accessible message.

Preparing the church

If you have a large cross for use as part of the walk of witness that may follow the service, place it at the front of church with a simple piece of paper attached to it, saying 'For me'. You might also like to have cards around the church with pictures of those who do things for us, e.g. a teacher, with the message 'They taught me', a policeman with 'They keep me safe', parents with 'They helped me to grow up', etc. Similar ideas could be used for an acetate or on a rolling PowerPoint presentation.

Beginning

In welcoming everyone say that Good Friday can be a difficult story to understand because Jesus did something for us that is hard to get our minds around.

Songs

Good Friday is often challenging, musically speaking, as lively songs and hymns are inappropriate. 'There is a green hill', 'When I survey' and 'Lift high the cross' are reasonably accessible to all ages. Modern songs such as: 'How deep the Father's love for us', 'Overwhelmed by love' and 'My Lord, what love is this?' are equally appropriate. Do not be afraid to use some quiet music before, during or after the service, to encourage the idea that this is not like other services, because Good Friday is not like other days.

Short talk 1

Ask who has received help today, and if so, how? Possible answers may include parents (hopefully!) or someone who has been helped across a road, helped to find out what time the service is or people who have been helped by being shown to their seat or given the books in church. Say that lots of people help us but very often we don't realise it and we fail to acknowledge it by saying thank you. Also, say that very often people do things for us without us realising it (e.g. road sweepers, hospital staff, police and other emergency services).

Say that you are going to hear some thoughts about one man who was there on the first Good Friday and that it must have been hard for him to watch a friend die. Joseph of Arimathea is one of those characters in the gospel stories who has a significant part to play but who never speaks. A member of the Sanhedrin, which was like the government of the day, we are told that he was 'Waiting for the Kingdom of God' and did not consent to the decision of the council to order Jesus' crucifixion (Luke 23:50, 51).

In those days, rich people would arrange to have their grave prepared a long time before they died so that they could make sure it was done properly. Joseph had done just that and so it was a brave decision on his part to ask Pilate for Jesus' body: he risked being made an outcast by the people around him and the end of any political ambitions he might have had.

Reading from the Bible

Read John 19:16-30 and 38-42, using a modern translation such as *The Message*. It would be good to have a number of readers, maybe spread around the church with short gaps for thought during the reading. Afterwards, have a short time of quiet (or some quiet music), and then someone will come forward to speak ...

Sketch

It would be good for the reader to read the references to Joseph before reading this in order to try and get inside the mind of the character. If he/she can learn the text, even better, but these are the thoughts of a deeply sad man and need to be read with expression and thoughtfulness as he stands, watches and thinks about what has happened. There are no props required but an image **(OHP 8)** of a tomb with the stone rolled in front of it could be an additional aspect to this sketch (but is not necessary for it to be effective).

The Kingdom has come, I know it, but I don't understand.
　　(Pause)
I didn't want it to happen.
Oh, no, I voted against it.
And spoke against the decision with all my might.
He was innocent.
He was the one we had waited for.
The Kingdom has come, I know it, but I don't understand.
　　(Pause)

The women have done their bit.
The Marys and Salome looked after him
every step of the way here,
but they can do no more.
It is my turn now.
They looked after him in life,
I must look after him in death.
The Kingdom has come, I know it, but I don't understand.
   (Pause)
Decades ago I chose the place,
and I watched them chisel this place out:
day after day, week after week,
blistered hands and breaking backs
to create the space.
The place where I wanted to be laid to rest.
But now there is no rest:
I seek a purpose, a reason, a hope in all of this.
The Kingdom has come, I know it, but I don't understand.
   (Pause)
My tomb has become his tomb.
But then he has taken my place in death.
The Kingdom has come, I know it, but I don't understand.
   (Pause)
I stand and watch.
And wait.
   (Pause)
The Kingdom is coming,
I know it,
But I don't understand.
   (He walks away)

Short talk 2

A short moment of quiet (or music) should follow the sketch. Follow this with a few brief thoughts ...

- Lots of people have done things for us.
- Very often we don't realise what people have done for us.
- Often we don't understand what people have done for us.
- Joseph knew that something had happened and that Jesus had done something for him – but he didn't know what or how.
- Joseph simply had to trust.
- We now know what Jesus did for us: Romans 5:8 'But God demonstrates his own love for us in this: While we were still sinners, Christ died for us.' **(OHP 9)**.
- Jesus died to take away the sin of the world – he did something very special for us on the Cross.
- The question is 'Do we realise how important that is?'

Statement of what we believe

Use the Affirmation of Faith number 4 on page 147 of *Common Worship,* saying that it tells us about what Jesus did for us.

Prayer of Repentance and Absolution

The responsive General Confession on page 124 of *Common Worship* and an Absolution such as the second one on page 135 are appropriate.

Intercessions and Lord's Prayer

Include prayers that show awareness and appreciation of those who do things for us and ask God to make us grateful for what they do. Especially thank God for what Jesus did for us and for the love which made it happen. Ask that others would begin to understand what Jesus did for them through the way we live our lives.

Ending

If there is a walk of witness after the service it may be appropriate to have the cross lead everyone out of the church. It may be appropriate to invite any who have begun to think about what Jesus did for them to talk over any issues which may have been raised with the clergy or a friend.

Watching
and
waiting

'But God demonstrates his
own love for us in this:
While we were still sinners,
Christ died for us.'

Romans 5:8

Easter Sunday

Are you sure? – John 20:1-18

- **What is the one thing you want them to take away?**

✓ That believing in the Resurrection is not as hard as it seems.

- **What is the one issue you want to challenge them about?**

✓ Do you believe even though you haven't seen?

- **What is the one thing you want them to apply in their lives?**

✓ That we live with many things that we cannot see yet believe in.

Like the work of the Holy Spirit, believing in the Resurrection involves accepting something that we cannot see, and yet it is something we can the effects of around us. If only we can get our minds around the simple step of 'What if it were true . . .?' then we can possibly get to a point of believing. Understanding 'why' is another question and, in some ways, is unimportant in the early stages of belief. Like those first disciples in the reading, for some it is simply important to 'believe' . . . 'Then the other disciple, who reached the tomb first, also went in, and he saw and believed; for as yet they did not understand the scripture, that he must rise from the dead.' (John 20:8, 9).

Preparing the church

Many churches will have been prepared to celebrate Easter with a considerable number of bright flowers and it would be good to draw attention to these (as well as those who have arranged them) – but be careful not to put things in front of them. Have a selection of A4 notices around the church with contrasting statements such as 'He's Alive!' and 'He's Alive?', 'New Life!' and 'New Life?', 'Resurrection!' and 'Resurrection?' An additional one with 'Are You Sure?' **(OHP 10)** could also be used as an OHP for before the service and as a backdrop to the talk. If you are using a digital projector, use a series of Easter-related images, such as clip art or flowers, eggs, etc., interspersed with these statements.

Beginning

Ask everyone what day it is! When they (hopefully!) respond with Easter Day, ask 'Are you sure?' Ask what happened on Easter Day and when told that it is the day Jesus rose from the dead ask: 'Are you sure?'

Say that you believe it to be true and that this is why you are all there today – but sometimes it is good to ask ourselves the question 'Are you sure?' to make sure we actually do believe.

Then use the Easter greeting of 'Christ is risen!' with the response 'He is risen indeed!' said three times, with the emphasis changing each time, leading straight into the first hymn.

Songs

'Jesus Christ is risen today' is a great hymn to start an Easter Day service and its very title is a statement of faith! Songs specifically aimed at children include 'This is the day', 'Thank you, Jesus' and, if it is used regularly in the local school, 'Lord of the Dance' may be useful. The quieter 'Sing hallelujah to the Lord' could be used to introduce the intercessions. 'In Christ alone' is a very good modern hymn that could be used, although 'Thine be the glory' is the usual hymn to bring an Easter service to a close!

Short talk 1

Play a brief 'True or False' game, asking which of the following are true . . .

- In 1977, David and Kym Barger carried an 8lb 15oz brick, without gloves, in a downward pincher hold for 45 miles.
- A man called Alfred West succeeded in splitting human hair into 18 pieces, longways.
- A Russian, Lieutenant Chisov, fell just under 22,000ft without a parachute and survived.
- Rev Donald Thomas of New York preached non-stop for 93 hours in May, 1979.
- A Frenchman called Monsieur Lotito once ate a whole bicycle – tyres, frame and all – in 15 days.

Say that, according to the *Guinness Book of Records*, they are all true. Then make a few, say five, statements about yourself of which one or more is incorrect. Make them as wacky as you can – but most people have done some amazing things at one time or another. If you know of someone in the congregation who has done some amazing things, you might want to make them the 'subject', rather than yourself. Ask the congregation which of the 'facts' are true and which are not. It may be good if you can ask your husband or wife, or a good friend, they know the answer – you may need to prime them! Ask the question 'Are you sure?' about the statements from the *Guinness Book of Records* and those about yourself (or the 'subject'). Say that, in each case, the truth relies on trust – trusting the book that those who witnessed the events are telling the truth, and those around you trusting either what they saw or what you told them. We trust that what we are told is true. Say that faith in God is about believing things that we are told and trusting that they are true – and you will come back to this later.

Prayer of Repentance

Use the 'Resurrection' Confession on page 125 of *Common Worship*, saying that it reminds us of the times when we have not trusted in God and done things his way. The last Absolution on page 135 is appropriate.

Reading from the Bible

Read John 20:1-18 from any modern translation. It is easily possible to dramatise the reading, using a narrator and people going to a 'tomb'.

Teaching

Remind everyone that you have said that believing in God and, in particular, believing in the Resurrection (what we mean when we say that Jesus came back to life on Easter Day) relies on us trusting what we are told – in particular, trusting that the story you have just had read is true.

Remind everyone of who was in the story: John (the 'other disciple' in the reading) and Peter, who went to the tomb but didn't actually see Jesus at that time, and Mary, who did! If, at that time, John, Peter and Mary had been asked the question 'Are you sure?' how do you think they would have reacted? Mary was convinced, because she had spoken to Jesus – but John and Peter would have probably said they 'believed' but didn't understand how it all fitted together because they had only seen an empty tomb and not met Jesus, like Mary had done. We are told that later on that day they *did* see Jesus, and believed fully.

Point out (mainly for the adults) that verses 8 and 9 tell us they believed but did not understand – and that it is OK for us to believe and accept that Jesus did rise from the dead even though we don't fully understand why.

Say that this is true in many parts of life – point out the beautiful flowers in church and ask what those flowers looked like a few weeks earlier. Say that they were only bulbs and didn't look anything like they do today – and say that the gardener who grew them trusted that they would grow, because she or he had been told by other people that they would and that they had seen pictures of what the flowers would finally look like.

Say that you can never 'prove' the resurrection – but, in the same way that people trust the eyewitness accounts of daft things in the *Guinness Book of Records,* or they trust that you are telling the truth about what you have done in your life, often without understanding them, so we can believe what we read in the Bible, because we can trust those who wrote it.

Statement of what we believe

Creed 1 on page 144 of *Common Worship* is ideal as the responses are 'We believe and trust in him'.

Intercessions and Lord's Prayer

Say that there are many in the world who do not believe or trust in God, and many do not believe in anything. Focus your prayers on asking that people in a variety of situations, international, national or local, will believe that God is there and trust that he will help them.

After a Final Hymn, an Ending

After a traditional Easter Blessing, use the response: 'Go in peace to believe and trust, and love and serve the risen Lord.'

'In the name of Christ, Amen.'

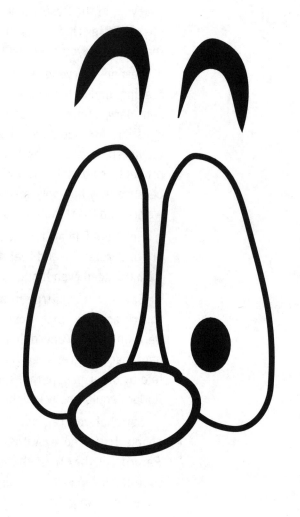

Are you sure?

Pentecost Sunday

You only need to ask! –
Acts 2:1-12

- **What is the one thing you want them to take away?**
- ✓ That we have to ask for more of the Holy Spirit.

- **What is the one issue you want to challenge them about?**
- ✓ Do you really want the Holy Spirit to work in your life?

- **What is the one thing you want them to apply in their lives?**
- ✓ An awareness of the need for the Holy Spirit and the need to keep asking.

The work of the Holy Spirit is a subject which many find hard to talk about. Many are comfortable with the idea that when we become Christians the Holy Spirit comes into our lives and is there, happily bubbling away in the background.

The question is whether we want the Holy Spirit to do more in our lives and, if so, how can we make it happen. The simple answer is in John 14:16, where Jesus says that he will ask the Father to send the Holy Spirit, and in Matthew 7:7 where Jesus says: 'Ask and it will be given to you.' The story of Pentecost in Acts 2 follows on from 10 days of prayer after Jesus' ascension when, I feel sure, there were plenty of prayers asking God to fulfil his promise to send the Spirit!

Preparing the church

The one investment needed for this service is a large bar of chocolate – the larger the bar, the better! The aim is that this sits in a prominent place, waiting for someone to ask for it – but no mention is made of it until the talk. In other words, it is there, but no one has asked for it (a bit like the Holy Spirit!).

You could also use the acetate with the big eyes looking towards the chocolate **(OHP 11)**, and you could have A4 cards around the church, listing the fruit and gifts of the Spirit, with single words on each card, e.g. 'Love' or 'Prophecy' (Galatians 5:16-25).

Beginning

Welcome everyone with a reminder that it is Pentecost, and a question to ask if anyone knows what is special about Pentecost – the day the Holy Spirit came and the day when the Church was born. You may like to sing Happy Birthday to yourselves: 'Happy Birthday to you/To Jesus be true/God bless you and keep you/Happy Birthday to you'.

Say that the church began with just a few dozen people (maybe as many as yourselves) and that it grew to be an enormous number of people – and today you are going to find out how that happened.

Songs

There are plenty of songs appropriate for Pentecost and 'Seek ye first', 'You said' and 'Give me oil in my lamp (Sing hosanna)' are particularly appropriate. Thoughtful songs such as 'Purify my heart', 'Be still for the presence of the Lord' and 'Holy Spirit, we welcome you' may be useful. 'O breath of life' or 'Breathe on me, breath of God' are traditional hymns that could be used.

Short talk

Ask if anyone has noticed anything in church this morning and when someone points out the chocolate, say that you hadn't noticed. Ask if it had been there all along and develop the conversation along the lines of 'Are you sure?', 'When did you spot it?', etc. Eventually leave the matter, saying that it is very nice that it is there and that you hope everyone enjoys looking at it. You *may* get the question 'Can I have it?' (probably from a child who has fewer inhibitions than the adults!) and let the conversation flow naturally through 'Why do you want it?' to 'What would you do with it?' If this question doesn't come, don't worry ... it can be used at the start of the teaching! If it does come, say that *maybe* they can have it later – but they will have to wait.

Reading from the Bible

Read Acts 2:1-12 from *The Message* or another modern translation, making sure whoever reads has practised the list of places! It could be read by a group of people spread round the church, shouting out the list of places and asking the question at the end of verse 12 together.

Teaching

If nobody asked for the chocolate earlier, remind people that you have it in the service and wonder out loud what you could do with it. When someone asks for it say 'Fine – all you had to do was ask!' but ask them what they intend to do with it. Ask a leading question: 'Are you going to eat it all by yourself?' with a view to encouraging them to share it.

Ask who noticed the chocolate before the service. How did you know it was there?

Ask who noticed that the Holy Spirit is with you in the service this morning . How did you know that he is there?

Say that the Holy Spirit is there with you just as much (if not more!) than the chocolate but it is easier to see chocolate – we have to look for the Holy Spirit and we see him through what the Spirit *does*. It's a bit like if you took the wrapper off the chocolate and hid it, it would still be there but you would only be able to smell it rather than be able to see it.

So we know the chocolate – and the Holy Spirit – is with you, but now what? (Hopefully, someone will say that now you eat the chocolate!)

Remember what I said to (the name of the person who asked for the chocolate)?

'All you had to do was ask for it.' The same is true of the Holy Spirit. He is here with us, and, in the same way, God wants us to simply ask for the Holy Spirit. (Put up **OHP 12** – 'You only need to ask!')

Remember Matthew 7:7-11, where it says: 'Ask and it will be given to you; seek and you will find; knock and the door will be opened to you. For everyone who asks receives; he who seeks finds; and to him who knocks, the door will be opened. Which of you, if his son asks for bread, will give him a stone? Or if he asks for a fish, will give him a snake? If you, then, though you are evil, know how to give good gifts to your children, how much more will your Father in heaven give good gifts to those who ask him!'

God wants us to ask him for the Holy Spirit to help us grow as Christians. He wants to make us more like Jesus with the same kind of love, joy, peace and all the other wonderful parts to Jesus' character. These are called the Fruit of the Spirit and the Holy Spirit helps us to be more like Jesus. How do we get the Holy Spirit? (Point out the OHP again: 'You only need to ask!')

God wants his church to grow and he gives people amazing gifts – special abilities that they didn't have before, to help the church to grow. These are called the gifts of the Spirit – how do we get them? Point to the OHP again: 'You only need to ask!'

Go to the story of Pentecost that you heard earlier and remind people that Jesus had gone back to be with his Father 10 days earlier. Ask if anyone knows what the disciples had been doing during that time? Show the second acetate **(OHP 13),** Acts 1:14 'They (that is the disciples) all joined together constantly in prayer, along with the women and Mary the mother of Jesus, and with his brothers.' What do you think they prayed for?

Jesus had promised that he would ask God to send the Holy Spirit – so it is probable that they were asking him to do just that. Finally say that God still gives people the Holy Spirit – and everyone who asks Jesus to be their Saviour has the Holy Spirit living inside them. But we need to ask God for more of the Holy Spirit every day, to give us the fruits (so that we are more like Jesus) and the gifts (so that the church will grow). How do we do it? Point to the OHP: 'You only need to ask!'

Statement of what we believe

The Creed based on Ephesians 3, number 7 on page 148 of *Common Worship* is suitable.

Prayer of Repentance

It may be better to put the Confession later in the service, saying that we have failed to do the one thing that God wants us to, namely to ask for his help. Instead, we have taken our eyes off God and done our own thing. The General Confession on page 128 of *Common Worship* with the fourth Absolution on page 136 may be suitable.

Intercessions and Lord's Prayer

Remind everyone that 'You only need to ask' for the Holy Spirit. Pray that God will send the Holy Spirit more and more into your church and every church, so that people will grow to be more like Jesus and that they will use their gifts so that the Church will grow. Ask that the Holy Spirit will also be there for those who are in difficult situations, whether they are important international problems or those who are ill or in difficulty near where you live.

Ending

As you leave, ask God to give the Holy Spirit, just like he promised.

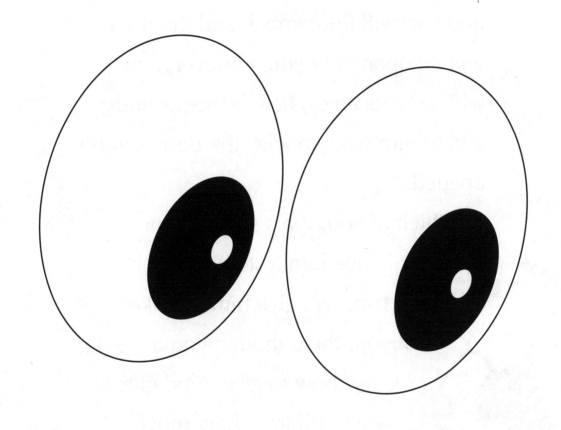

'You only need to ask'

Matthew 7:7-11

'Ask and it will be given to you; seek and you will find; knock and the door will be opened to you. For everyone who asks receives; he who seeks finds; and to him who knocks, the door will be opened.

'Which of you, if his son asks for bread, will give him a stone? Or if he asks for a fish, will give him a snake?

'If you, then, though you are evil, know how to give good gifts to your children, how much more will your Father in Heaven give good gifts to those who ask him!'

'You only need to ask'

Acts 1:14

'They (that is the Disciples) all joined together constantly in prayer, along with the women and Mary the mother of Jesus, and with his brothers.'

What do you think they prayed for?

Trinity Sunday

Why are we here? – Matthew 28:16-20

- **What is the one thing you want them to take away?**
- ✓ We are engaged in a mission for God.

- **What is the one issue you want to challenge them about?**
- ✓ Why are we here?

- **What is the one thing you want them to apply in their lives?**
- ✓ To actively engage in being a disciple and to make new ones.

This service is not about trying to understand the Trinity – other books in this series have grappled with those issues! This service is about asking what the church is actually for. For some it is a place to worship and meet with God, for others it is a place of refuge and for others it is a club of people who happen to be Christians. There are many different answers and, to some extent, each of them has an element of truth in them. The one answer, which Jesus gave, is: 'The Great Commission' of Matthew 28:20 – our job is to encourage the next generation of the church to follow Jesus and this challenges us to follow him for ourselves in order that they may do so, too. This is a particularly good service to include a Baptism!

Preparing the church

Put up **OHP 14** with the question 'What's The Job?' If you have a digital projector, find photos or clipart of a variety of well-known jobs and intersperse the slides with a slide saying 'What's The Job ?'

Beginning

Invite the congregation to greet each other using the Trinitarian handshake – 'I greet you in the name of the Father (shake once in a normal fashion but don't let go), the Son (twist your hands so that your thumb is vertical whilst grasping the other hand) and the Holy Spirit (maintaining the grip, wave your fingers at each other). It is not as difficult as it sounds (and if you did it in Years B and C, it should be easy by now!)

Songs

There is a need to mix traditional Trinity hymns with hymns thinking about outreach in this service. 'Holy, holy, holy is the Lord', 'Holy, holy, Lord God Almighty' are appropriate, as are modern songs such as 'Rejoice' and 'We want to see Jesus lifted high'. Quieter songs to use could include 'Send me out from here, Lord' and 'There is a Redeemer '.

A short talk

Prime one or two people before the service to come up and talk about their work. Most of the people present will have some idea as to the jobs of those people – but if you have someone who is relatively unknown, you could easily turn this into a 'What's My Line?' quiz, which involves asking questions which can be answered only yes or no, and the congregation has to guess. Note also that this does not have to solely include those in paid employment – be ready to use those who do voluntary work as well!

When you have established their job you can follow this up with the following main questions:

- What do you do?
- Why do you do it?
- What skills do you need to do the job?
- Who tells you what to do?
- Who showed you how to do the job?

  This could easily become a regular part of the service – as a way of introducing the congregation to each other! Finish the time by praying for the people concerned, that they might do their job well and have all the resources to make a success of it.

Prayer of Repentance

The Confession on page 127 of *Common Worship* for 'City, World and Society' may need a little explanation but is appropriate, as is the second Absolution on page 136.

Reading from the Bible

Read Matthew 28:20, using a modern translation. One way of making it interesting would be to have two readers and a group of people to be the Disciples. The first reader, the Narrator, reads verses 16–18a and the Disciples gather around Jesus, who reads verses 18a–20. The Disciples then turn and go back into the body of the church.

Teaching

Explain that the reading you have just heard took place 40 days after Easter Day, just as Jesus was about to go back to heaven, to be with his Father. Ask a series of questions to find out what was happening (put up the OHP as a prompt – it will be needed later in the service, too):

- What was happening in that reading? (Jesus was telling his Disciples the job they had to do after he had gone.)
- What was the job? (To make disciples)
- Where were they to make disciples (Everywhere)
- What are disciples? (People who followed Jesus)
- Would they be doing it on their own? (No, Jesus promised to be with them)

Ask who will still be in the church in 100 years' time – say it is possible that one or two of the very youngest present might still be there, but there would need to be a whole new generation of Christians to be in the church in 100 years' time. These are people who need to hear about Jesus and decide to follow him – to become disciples, in the same way that you are all disciples. Ask how are they going to find out about Jesus and who is going to tell them – and help everyone to realise that this is 'The Job' we all have to do.

Remind everyone about the people you spoke to earlier and the jobs they did. Using the OHP you used earlier, ask the same questions about the 'Job' that Jesus gave us.

The first two questions are general ones that should get the conversation going:

- What do you do? (Tell people about Jesus by the way we live and the things we say).
- Why do you do it? (Because we want people to find out about how wonderful it is to have Jesus as our best friend and our Saviour).

The remaining three questions involve the Trinity (OHP 15):

- What skills do you need to do the job?
  Say that it is not an easy job and everyone needs help to learn the skills – say that this is why the Holy Spirit came: to help us in the job God has given us to do. The Holy Spirit can help us by guiding the things we say and helping us to know what to do.
- Who tells you what to do ?
  Ask who our boss is. Say it is God who wants the job to be done, and that Jesus said in verse 18: 'All authority has been given to me', meaning that God told him what to tell the Disciples – in other words: God is 'the Boss'.
- Who showed you how to do the job ?
  Jesus went around telling people about God and encouraging them to become disciples – so the best way for us to learn the job is to become more and more like Jesus.

Remind everyone that today is Trinity Sunday – a day when we realise that there are different aspects to God's character that we see as Father, Son and Holy Spirit and that when we look at what God wants us to be doing, we see God as the one who tells us what we should be doing, Jesus is the one who shows us how it should be done and the Holy Spirit is there to help us with the job.

And we must never forget that we are not doing the job on our own – remember Jesus' final words: 'I am with you always' – and that means now!

Statement of what we believe

Creed 7 on page 148 of *Common Worship* shows the work of the Trinity and reinforces the message of the talk.

Intercessions and Lord's Prayer

Focus your prayers on the job that God has called us to do:

- For those who are missionaries or evangelists, doing what God wanted them to do and telling people across the world about his love.
- For those who work with children and young people and encourage them to be disciples.
- For each one in church today that they may take the job we have been given seriously.
- Also thank God that he is mysterious and that we cannot understand the Trinity!
- Thank God the Father for being 'the Boss' and ask that we may do what he wants us to do.
- Thank God the Son, Jesus, for showing us how to do the job.
- And thank God the Holy Spirit for the ways he helps us to do the job.

Ending

Repeat the Trinitarian handshake but this time as a blessing – 'God bless you in the name of the Father (shake once in a normal fashion but don't let go), the Son (twist your hands so that your thumb is vertical whilst grasping the other hand) and the Holy Spirit (maintaining the grip, wave your fingers at each other). Go for it!

What's the job?

- What do you do?
- Why do you do it?
- What skills do you need to do the job?
- Who tells you what to do?
- Who showed you how to do the job?

God the Father

(The one who tells us
what we should be doing)

God the Son,
Jesus

(The one who
shows us how to do it)

God the
Holy Spirit

(The one who
helps us do it)

Father's Day

And there's more –
Ephesians 3:14-21; Luke 15:11-24a

- **What is the one thing you want them to take away?**
- ✓ That there is no end to the love of God the Father.

- **What is the one issue you want to challenge them about?**
- ✓ Have we learnt to live without fathers – including God?

- **What is the one thing you want them to apply in their lives?**
- ✓ To have the confidence and freedom to live life with a loving father.

It is probably no exaggeration that Father's Day is promoted most heavily by the card industry and it flies in the face of reality as far as society is concerned. For many, both outside and inside the church, the issue of fatherhood has been sidelined in the light of the changing family. Many church, as well as non-church families grow up without a father and, as a result, people shy away from the subject in the well-meaning but mistaken desire not to offend. This service aims to acknowledge clearly that for many, fatherhood is a difficult subject, with bad relationships or abuse causing pain and long-term separation – but to acknowledge, also, the infinite and pure love of our Heavenly Father. There is no doubt that for some wives and children, both young and 'adult' children, this is a difficult subject, but it is right to affirm those who are desperately trying to be the fathers God wants them to be, as well as to understand that in the absence of an earthly father, we have a heavenly Father who will *never* let us down.

It may be a good idea to promote this service as a special one for Father's Day.

Preparing the church

If you have an OHP available, prepare a slide with the words 'A Loving Dad?' on it. If you have access to a PowerPoint presentation using a projector, find some photos of well-known dads and show a rolling display of them with the question 'A loving dad?' under each one. They do not have to be *good* parents in anyone's eyes and it may be good to include those who have struggled in some way or another.

Beginning

Welcome everyone, especially any dads or grandfathers present. Say that being a father isn't always easy and some do not manage to remain part of their families. Say, also, that there are bad fathers as well as good fathers and that everyone present will have an idea of what makes a good or a bad father. Today you want everyone to realise that however good or bad their father has been, we have in God the best Father anyone could ever want. (Be careful to make this beginning as succinct as possible, using, if possible, a script in your own words for it – this is important as everyone needs to understand that you are not ignoring realities in society but pointing to realities in eternity!)

Songs

There are many songs that refer to the Fatherhood of God, including 'Abba, Father', 'God is our Father', 'Father, I can call you Father', or 'Father God, I wonder', although it may be sensible to change some words about 'sonship' to childhood (e.g. in the last of these songs) as some songs were not written in the language of the current time! Hymns such as 'O Father of the fatherless', 'Great is thy faithfulness' or 'How deep the Father's love for us' may also be helpful.

Reading 1

It would be good to have the reading from Ephesians (3:14-21) read nearer the start of the service, perhaps in between two songs about the love of God the Father.

Short talk

Researchers asked 500 children about their parents, covering 36 categories which compared mums with dads. Dads don't come out too well! In 35 out of 36, mums are better, according to those surveyed. Guess which category dads won. They're better drivers, apparently! Teenagers between 15-18, however, give dads a higher rating than younger kids for 'Respects my privacy', 'Keeps his word' and 'Has a good sense of humour'. It seems dads gradually learn!

Ask who is the most famous dad in the world? Some may say a famous person such as David Beckham or a pop star, but the most famous dad is probably Homer Simpson – who, in many ways, is a failure in everything he tries to be. But people like him because he keeps trying to do the right thing.

The wonderful thing about God the Father is that he always does the right thing. Remind everyone of the reading you heard earlier from Ephesians – that Paul wanted, above everything else, for his friends in Ephesus to know how enormous God's love is. Ask the children how big they think God's love is . . . As big as the room? As big as the world? As big as space? Say it is impossible to get to the end of God's love – read again verses 17b to 19 and say that Paul wanted his friends to live their lives so that they never, ever doubted God's love for them. After a song, say that you are going to hear a story of how great that love is . . .

Reading 2

The second reading, telling the story of the Prodigal Son in Luke 15:11-24a, could be told by three voices – narrator, father and son, using the pulpit or the back of the church as places for father and son to read from. Encourage the father to run down the aisle! You could, instead of or as well as using the reading, use the sketch 'The Story of the Fantastic Father' in *Conversations on the Way* by this author. (Kevin Mayhew, 2001, ISBN 1 84003 730 X, Cat No. 1500427).

Song

A more modern song, such as 'How deep the Father's love for us', would be appropriate at this stage.

Prayer of Repentance

It may be good to have the reading from Luke as an introduction to the confession, explaining that fathers may not always be good, but then neither are children! All of us have behaved like the son in Jesus' story and need to 'go home' and say sorry to God our Father. The Confession at the bottom of page 127 in *Common Worship* is, not surprisingly, the best one! The fourth Absolution on page 135 is also appropriate.

Teaching

Ask some questions:

- How much of the father's money did the younger son go off with? (Half)
- How much did he spend? (All of it!)
- Why didn't he go home straight away? (Feeling guilty, foolish, silly and a failure)
- Do you think his father was cross with him? (Sad rather than cross, but greater than both of these was his love).

Explain that in Jesus' time, a father was a very great figure who would walk very slowly everywhere and certainly would not run. So when Jesus told the story, people would have laughed at the fact that the father ran *and* that the father would have wanted to forgive his son. Ask what is the one thing we should do when we have hurt someone or done wrong (say sorry). Ask if it is easy to forgive people when they have hurt you – most children will be more honest than the grown-ups and say it is very hard! Ask what is the one thing we need in order to forgive people (love) and ask people to imagine how much love God must have to forgive everyone who does something wrong and then comes to say sorry.

Remind people how great is God's love (Ephesians 3) and then say the Bible also tells us, 'If we confess our sins, he is faithful and just and will forgive us our sins and purify us from all unrighteousness' (1 John 1:9), which means: 'If we say sorry to him, God will forgive us.'

That is how much our Father God loves us – enough to forgive us absolutely everything. Finally, ask this question. Do your parents only love you when you say sorry (no, they love you all the time) – so if God loves us when we say sorry, he must love us *all* the time! That's an amazing thought! Sum up that thought in a prayer.

Statement of what we believe

Creed 7 on page 148 of *Common Worship* is appropriate, as it is taken from Ephesians 3.

Intercessions and Lord's Prayer

If you wanted to have a period of quiet, someone could sing 'The Father's song' by Matt Redman as an introduction. Focus your prayers on the need for people to know that they are loved by God – and amongst your prayers . . .

- Give thanks for fathers and grandfathers present and pray that they will be good fathers.
- Pray for those who do not have a father, who are separated from their father or do not know who their father is – pray that they will know just how much God loves them and wants to be their father.
- Pray for those who are 'famous' fathers as well as fathers whose jobs often take them away from home – pray that they will be able to juggle their time in the right way.

Ending

In your final prayer, draw together the themes of the service, giving thanks for God's immense love as well as thanking him for his forgiveness and the fact that he will never let us down. You may want to give a present to all the men in the congregation (such as a chocolate!) and a card with Ephesians 3:14-18 on it.

Service in Advent

Growing the Harvest –
Psalm 8; Matthew 13:1-9

- **What is the one thing you want them to take away?**

✓ That when we come to Harvest, we come to say thanks for a process that began a long time ago.

- **What is the one issue you want to challenge them about?**

✓ That modern thinking expects instant results.

- **What is the one thing you want them to apply in their lives?**

✓ To see that the Christian life, like the harvest, involves long-term growth.

The culture of twenty-first-century Britain (and the rest of the western world, for that matter) is involved with an expectation of instantaneous results. Companies and politicians alike know that their investors and voters expect them to achieve significant results within a short space of time. Everything is about being faster and more efficient – and this extends to the production of food. The desire for GM crops is often driven by a desire for increased production in a shorter space of time. Involved in Jesus' parable of the sower was an awareness of the need to grow in the right place, at the right time and in the right way – and he warned against quick growth without roots. In this service there is a twin approach of giving thanks for the process which has brought about the Harvest gifts but also to reassure the congregation (of all ages) that growth takes time!

Preparing the church

If you have an OHP available, prepare a slide with the words 'Instant Harvest' on it **(OHP 16)**. If you have access to a PowerPoint presentation using a projector, find (or take!) pictures of a variety of instant products that are on the market today – e.g. dried food, 'TV dinners' or packaged 'easy' meals.

Beginning

Welcome people and invite everyone to be quiet for a moment. In the quiet, arrange for someone to read Psalm 8. If you have a microphone, so that the voice is 'disembodied', so much the better. If you have a projector, put up a slide of a wheat field – if you have digital facilities, put up several slides of natural food production, such as crops or animals.

Songs

Immediately after reading Psalm 8, it would be good to simply say: 'Today is a day when we remember how good God has been to us,' and lead straight into the song

'God is good'. At this point, a bigger welcome (along with brief notices) may be offered and the congregation invited to stand and sing 'We plough the fields and scatter', while harvest gifts are brought forward. The traditional hymn 'Come, ye thankful people, come' might also be used, but other songs such as 'Give thanks', or 'Who paints the skies?' are also suitable. The modern words of 'For the fruits of his creation' to the traditional tune Ar Hyd Y Nos (otherwise known as 'All through the night') makes a good alternative.

Prayer of Repentance

Say a word of thanks for the gifts and then have the Confession to remind us that we often take for granted what God has given us. The Harvest Confession on page 126 of *Common Worship* and the second Absolution on page 135 are appropriate.

Short talks

Have available a selection of the 'instant' food seen at the beginning of the service and ask if anyone notices what is special about these foods (they require little preparation).

Ask what other similar non-instant foods are available (e.g. potatoes as opposed to instant mashed potato) and ask how long they take to grow. Remind everyone that the farmers began preparing the fields after last year's harvest and will have ploughed and sown seed in the spring, keeping a careful eye throughout the summer in readiness for harvesting at the right time.

Ask: 'Who made the food grow?' (The answer, hopefully, will be God!) Argue for a moment, saying that surely it was the farmer who made the food grow, after all, he or she did all the work. Tease out the understanding that it is God who makes the food grow and so that is why we come to church to say thank you to him (as well as to the farmers for all their work).

Reading from the Bible

Read Matthew 13:1-9. If you have a variety of voices available, read it from a dramatised version or from *The Message*. You may like to have some children around the church playing the different parts (e.g. the growing seed, the birds carrying the seed off, or the weeds strangling the growing plants – but be careful of overzealous weeds!)

Sketch

The following sketch could be used to illustrate the point of the service (if it is used, the dramatic form of the reading may be less necessary). It is a simple conversation between an interviewer and an eccentric professor – and the props are simple, too. An OHP with the title 'Gardening for Geeks' could be used **(OHP 17)**, but apart from that, keep it simple! The interviewer can be dressed in jacket and tie, equipped with microphone and clipboard and the professor can be dressed in as bizarre manner as possible!

Interviewer	Welcome to 'Gardening for Geeks' – the show where we look at the latest theories that you can put into practice in your own garden.
	Tonight I am pleased to welcome Professor Theophilus P. Rhubarb, who claims to have a revolutionary new approach to growth.
	Professor Rhubarb, let's start at the beginning - what is the problem you have attempted to solve?
Rhubarb	Well, it's very simple, really. Like millions of other people, I get very impatient at the slow way all the stuff in my garden grows.
	I don't want to sit around all day with nothing there! I want excitement! I want bright colours! And I want them NOW.
Interviewer	But what about the products that already exist to improve growth?
Rhubarb	Well, they're all very well – but they are still too slow.
	I mean, some of them say you have to wait as long as a month - a month, I tell you, before there is any sign of growth.
Interviewer	So your work is, I suppose, involved with trying to accelerate this growth?
Rhubarb	That's correct.
Interviewer	And how have you gone about this?
Rhubarb	Well, the theory hangs on the phrase: 'A little of what you like does you good'.
	My hypothesis was to extend this to: 'A lot of what you like will do a heck of a lot of stuff'.
Interviewer	I see – and how did this hypothesis work in practice?
Rhubarb	Well, my initial work involved physical growth: I like things like Chinese takeaway food and lager, so I experimented with the idea by living on three takeaways and 10 pints of lager a day.
Interviewer	And . . .
Rhubarb	And it was very successful: I proved that an excess of food would lead to substantial growth.
Interviewer	Very interesting . . . and how did things progress from there?
Rhubarb	Well, when I hit 25 stone the doctor persuaded me that this was not a long-term solution and that I ought to think it through further.
Interviewer	So . . .
Rhubarb	I applied it to economics.
Interviewer	Tell me more.
Rhubarb	Well, working on the principle that there is something in all the special offers that come through my door each day I decided to try one of them out. I wrote off to one that promised I could earn mountains of money by investing just a small amount with a company called 'Splash Your Cash Incorporated'.
Interviewer	And . . .
Rhubarb	Oh they certainly splashed my cash.
Interviewer	So there were good returns, were there?
Rhubarb	Well, so I gather – 'Splash Your Cash Incorporated' now owns several small islands in the Bahamas.
	They certainly got rich quick.
Interviewer	And you . . .
Rhubarb	Didn't.
Interviewer	I see, so have you tried anything else?
Rhubarb	Well, this is the interesting bit, because I have tried to apply this to gardening.
Interviewer	What, by putting Chinese takeaways and lager on your soil?

Rhubarb	No, not exactly, but by trying large amounts of manure, fertilisers and gardening products.
Interviewer	And ...
Rhubarb	And I can't actually tell you, because it smells so awful, I haven't got close enough to find out!
Interviewer	But any suspicions?
Rhubarb	Well, to be honest, I think I have proved something. It's quite fundamental, really.
Interviewer	Which is?
	(Pause)
Rhubarb	It doesn't work.
Interviewer	There's no quick fix?
Rhubarb	Exactly.
Interviewer	So there you have it ...
	'A little of what you like does you good' –
	but: 'A lot of what you like will do ...
	... absolutely nothing.' Goodnight!

Teaching

Draw together what you have learned so far:

- That it is God that makes things grow, not us.
- That things take a long time to grow.
- That we like things to be instantly available and we have to learn to be patient.
- That Jesus said that growing as a Christian takes time, too.

Remind the congregation of the Parable of the Sower **(OHP 18)**, and ask why some of the seed (and Christians) did not grow properly. Say what Jesus said the problems were (Matthew 13:18-22 has the answers!). Note that:

- The seed on the path represents people who think that following Jesus would be a good idea, but can't be bothered to actually do it.
- The seed on the rocky ground are people who think that following Jesus would be a good idea, and get very excited about it – but as soon as it becomes hard to be a Christian (e.g. people at school find out and make a few comments), they give up because they haven't kept going at it.
- The seed in the weeds are people who do stick at it for a while and then think that other things, like friends, money or possessions are more important – and give up.
- But the seed on the good soil are people who stick at it – who take time to grow and have roots that take up all the food they need to grow.

What makes us strong as Christians – what are the 'roots' of being a Christian? (Answer ... Reading the Bible, praying, going to church).

Conclude by reminding everyone that being a Christian, whether we are young or old, is about growing over a long period of time and that there are no 'quick' ways to grow as a Christian **(OHP 19)**. We need to stick at it, to have roots to get the things we need to grow – and if we do so, we will be like the seed in Jesus' story that produced lots of fruit at the end.

Statement of what we believe

Creed 7 on page 148 of *Common Worship* may be appropriate as it has a sense of growth and nurture throughout it.

Intercessions and Lord's Prayer

Focus prayers on long-term growth, including prayers:

- Giving thanks for the long-term work of farmers and those who work to improve the environment, that they may be committed to long-term benefits rather than short-term gain.
- For those in countries where the harvest fails, that their leadership would act wisely – and that countries like our own would be willing to share our vast resources with them.
- Giving thanks, too, for those who are responsible for our long-term growth as Christians, including those who teach in Sunday School or Youth Groups.
- That people in church, young and old, will grow in their faith day by day, and put down strong roots.

Ending

As a final prayer, draw the themes of the service together, giving thanks to God that the Harvest for next year is already growing and that he is a 'long-term' God who was, and is and always will be loving and patient, encouraging our growth.

Instant Harvest

'O Lord,
our Lord,
how majestic
is your name
in all the earth'

Psalm 8:1

The seed on the path . . .

The seed on the
rocky ground . . .

The seed in the weeds . . .

The seed in the good soil . . .

It is God who
makes things grow

Things take a long
time to grow

We like things to be
instantly available

Growing as a Christian
takes time

Service in the Sundays after Easter

The lakeside appearance – John 20:15-19

- **What is the one thing you want them to take away?**
- ✓ That a declaration of love is a changing point in any relationship.
- **What is the one issue you want to challenge them about?**
- ✓ 'Do you love me?'
- **What is the one thing you want them to apply in their lives?**
- ✓ To grow in our love for God and to understand more of what it means.

This service is based around a reading that can be used in the weeks after Easter Sunday. While not necessarily appropriate for Easter Sunday itself, it could be applied to a youth service in the evening of one of the Sundays following Easter – especially if it is a Baptismal service.

Modern-day life is immersed in the desire to talk about love – except that it is a concept of love which is far removed from the love God wants us to have from him. Twenty-first-century love is a mushy, emotional love which is characterised in songs and films and yet has little staying power. It is all about what the individual can get out of it, rather than what they can give to it. So when Jesus says to Peter: 'Do you love me?', we have many barriers to overcome – the barriers of language (mentioned in the talk) and the barriers of the meanings and connotations attached to the word love itself.

Preparing the church

If you have an OHP available, prepare a slide with the word 'Love' on it. If you have access to a digital projector put up a scrolling display of lyrics to well-known secular love songs.

Beginning

Welcome people and, if appropriate, use the Easter greeting: 'Alleluia, Christ is risen', to which the response from the congregation is: 'He is risen indeed. Alleluia.' Tell people that you are going to be thinking about love today and that, above all, the Easter story tells us about a special kind of love – the kind of love that God has for us and wants us to have for each other.

Songs

'Come on and celebrate', 'Your love is amazing' and 'Overwhelmed by love' are some of the many songs which might be appropriate. 'Lord, I lift your name on high' may make the connection between John 3:16 and the Easter story, and 'Before the throne of God above' may be an appropriate song with which to finish the service.

However, a theme of love may enable the church favourites to have an airing – or possibly to have rest!

Short talk

Ask people to name as many different pop songs as they can with the word love in the title, e.g. 'Love is a many splendoured thing', 'Love me tender', 'Love changes everything', 'All you need is love', 'I want to know what love is'. (It is amazing how many Beatles songs will appear in the list!) Ask what films people can think of which involve love, e.g. *The Sound of Music, Sleepless in Seattle, Notting Hill, Love Actually.* Ask why people like songs and films that are about love – and ask why love is so important. Ask if people know what Jesus said were the two most important things that people should do (Mark 12:29-31).

Prayer of Repentance

Ask if anyone knows the verse John 3:16 and if they know what it means. Say that it tells us that the main reason Jesus came was that God loves us, and the reason Jesus died on the cross for us was because he shared that love. If appropriate, use the Confession at the top of page 128 of *Common Worship*, explaining the picture of our love being like a cloud that fades away. The fourth Absolution on page 135 is an appropriate one.

Reading from the Bible

Read John 21:15-19. If you have a variety of voices available, read it from a dramatised version with one person being Jesus and one being Peter.

Teaching

Remind people that you are talking about love and recall the moment in the summer-house in *The Sound of Music* or the moment at the top of the Empire State Building in *Sleepless in Seattle* (or another film you may think of) when, at a crucial point in the film, one person expresses their love for the other – and then the orchestra hiding in the background suddenly bursts into life and, usually, what follows is a great big snog!

Say that expressing love in words is often very hard to do. But we want to hear it expressed and unless someone is prepared to say it, we wonder if they actually do, indeed, love us.

Jesus asked Peter: Do you love me? A simple enough question – but the answer is an enormous one. In a film, if one actor says: 'Do you love me?' the answer directs the whole of the film: 'Yes' equals orchestra and snog and 'no' nearly always means the end of relationship. In the story you have just heard, we hear Jesus asking Peter what he thinks of him.

It is as though Jesus is saying to him: 'You've seen everything.
You were there right at the beginning.
You saw me heal your mother-in-law.

You saw me bring Jairus' daughter and Lazarus back to life.
You saw me die on a cross.
You saw me – and you see me alive: right now.
So what do you think?
Do you love me?'

You can almost hear Peter's heart thumping as he debates how to answer. It's hard to know the exact wording of Jesus' questions: The original questions were in Aramaic and John wrote them in Greek and we read them in English! People have struggled to work out what was really said – maybe it was something like this:

'Peter – do you *love* me more than these?'
'Lord, you know that I *like* you.'
'Simon, son of John, do you *really love* me?'
'Lord, you know that I *really like* you.'
'Simon, son of John, do you *just have affection* for me, do you *just like* me?'
'Lord, you know all things; you know that I *love* you.'
Jesus was saying to Peter: 'Tell me how you feel about me and what I have done for you.'

Say that often we are like Peter – we are not sure how to react to Jesus and the question of whether we love him or not. Do we say 'yes' - and risk the consequences, or do we say 'no' and walk away, wondering what might have been the friendship we could have had with Jesus.

Jesus asks the same question of us – Do you love me?

For Peter it led to spending his life telling people about Jesus and, according to tradition, he died being crucified upside down in Rome.

Jesus asked Peter on the lakeside – Do you love me?

We can waffle on about not knowing what love means or thinking it means what songs or films tell us that love means. Or we can make excuses and use delaying tactics trying to water down the question – but, in the end, it is a question we must answer.

Statement of what we believe

Creed 1 on page 144 of *Common Worship* is appropriate as it is similar to the thoughts of John 3:16.

Intercessions and Lord's Prayer

Focus prayers on 'love':
- Pray that people might learn to love one another, not as in films and songs, but as God loves us.
- Pray that there would be love where so often love is missing: in countries where there is war and in divided communities around the world.
- Pray that those who are ill in any way would know God's love – and that we might find ways of showing them that love.
- Pray that we might have a growing love for God each day.

Ending

As a final prayer, ask the question that Jesus asked Peter and asks us. 'Do you love me?' and pray that each of us will be able to answer 'yes'. We may not know what it means and our love may be only tiny, but pray that our love will be there in response to his enormous love for us.

A Baptismal Service

You're special – Matthew 3:13-17

- **What is the one thing you want them to take away?**
✓ That everyone is special in God's eyes.

- **What is the one issue you want to challenge them about?**
✓ How do I think God feels about me?

- **What is the one thing you want them to apply in their lives?**
✓ To live with a relationship with God that does not involve guilt or fear.

Ask non-churched people what their concept of God is and they will often offer a picture of either the 'Insignificant God' who sits on a cloud and is completely irrelevant, or the 'Big Brother God', who is a complete control-freak and is responsible for all wars and suffering. Rarely will people have a sense of God who actually cares for them and loves them.

This service is aimed at providing an opportunity for those who come to church for a Baptismal service, to hear how God the Father felt about Jesus, and especially how that love might apply to not only the child at the centre of the service, but to his or her parents – and absolutely everyone. For the sake of ease and convenience, we have used the word *[Name]* whenever the candidate's name is referred to. Please remember to insert the correct name at the relevant points in your service!

Preparing the church

If you have an OHP available, use the slide with the words 'You are special' on it **(OHP 20)**. If you have access to a digital projector put up a display of slides with a developing message, changing every minute in the five minutes leading up to the start of the service. Begin with 'You are special!' following on with 'No, you really *are* special!', 'Yes, this means you … you are special!', 'Not the person sitting next to you, I mean you … you are special!' and finally 'You are incredibly, utterly, absolutely and totally special!'

Beginning

Welcome people, especially the family and friends of those connected to the Baptism party. And welcome *[Name]* – go and say: '*[Name]* – this is your special day and your special service. I hope you will grow up to know how special you are.'

Songs

It would help to concentrate the theme if it is possible to sing 'I'm special' at the start of the service, but local custom may make this impossible! Hymns such as 'Amazing grace' or 'And can it be?' may be appropriate to start and finish the service and other songs such as 'Your love is amazing' 'Blessed be the name of the Lord' or 'Such love' are some of the many songs which might be appropriate.

Sketch

Ask if anyone in the congregation has done anything wrong this week and be amazed when people admit they have! Say that you thought only perfect people came to church and then say that one reason we come to church is that we know that all of us do things wrong and all of us need to be forgiven. Say that you are going to listen to a sketch and then some words written by King David, about 3000 years ago.

How you might use this sketch
This is best performed with the three voices in a row – Voice 1 being in the middle. Voices 2 and 3 stand back until Voice 1 has finished and then stand either side, whilst Voice 1 bows their head and listens. And yes, Private Fraser is the voice for the '. . . doomed' line!

Voice 1

Oops, I've done it again.
A silly little mistake I know,
and I must stop doing it;
but, oops, I've done it again.

Or maybe . . .
maybe it wasn't an 'oops':
more of an 'Oh no!'

You see, an 'Oops' is almost insignificant.
Well, it seems insignificant to me.
I wonder what God thinks?

An 'Oh no!' is far more serious.
An 'Oh no!' is one of those things
that is just s-o-o-o embarrassing.

The sort of thing
which someone knows about
and makes me think, well, 'Oh no!'

I wonder what people think?
I wonder what God thinks?

Now I've done it . . . I'm doomed!
I have *really* gone and done it this time.
I'm doomed . . . *completely doomed!*

This time
I know what God thinks.

People will hate me
for what I've done.

God must hate me
for what I've done.

I know *I* hate me
for what I've done.

There's no way back this time.

It's not an 'Oops'
that doesn't really matter.

It's not an 'Oh no!'
that will pass in time.

This time 'I'm doomed'.

There's no way back;
God cannot possibly forgive me for this.

Voices 2 and 3

2   Have mercy on me, O God,
     according to your unfailing love;

3   according to your great compassion
     blot out my transgressions.

2   Wash away all my iniquity
     and cleanse me from my sin.

3   For I know my transgressions,
     and my sin is always before me.

2   Against you, you only,
     have I sinned and done what is evil in your sight,

3   so that you are proved right when you speak
     and justified when you judge.

2   Surely I was sinful at birth,
     sinful from the time my mother conceived me.

3   Surely you desire truth in the inner parts;
     you teach me wisdom in the inmost place.

2 Cleanse me with hyssop, and I shall be clean;
 wash me, and I shall be whiter than snow.

3 Let me hear joy and gladness;
 let the bones you have crushed rejoice.

2 Hide your face from my sins
 and blot out all my iniquity.

3 Create in me a pure heart, O God,
 and renew a steadfast spirit within me.

2 Do not cast me from your presence
 or take your Holy Spirit from me.

Prayer of Repentance

Remind everyone that Jesus came to deal with our sin – however big or small it may be. If appropriate, use the Responsive Confession at the bottom of page 128 of *Common Worship*. The last Absolution on page 136 is also appropriate.

The Baptism Liturgy

The Baptism Liturgy fits into the service at this point and includes a creed, the Lord's Prayer and prayers for *[Name]* and their family.

Reading from the Bible

Read Matthew 3:13-17 from a modern version of the Bible.

Teaching

(OHP 21) I'm special!

Remind people that you have talked about the fact that every one of us sins and needs to be washed clean on the inside in the same way as we need to wash the outside when we get dirty.

Remind them, too, that when you baptised *[Name]*, the water reminded us of the washing on the inside that we can have because of Jesus' death on the cross.

Ask people what makes them feel special. For children, it may be something like receiving a certificate at school or getting into the school team. For some it might be receiving flowers or chocolates. For others it might be getting a new job or receiving recognition for some work achievement. Although you may get some very good answers such as knowing that they are loved by their family and friends, say that most people only feel special when someone else notices that they have done something – if you have an example of winning something or achieving something, and others saw you receive this accolade, then please share it.

Remind everyone of the simple story that you have just heard – the story of Jesus' baptism. Make the following points:

(OHP 22) Jesus' baptism

- People got baptised by John as a sign to everyone that they wanted to be clean on the inside.

- John didn't want to baptise Jesus, because he knew he was already clean on the inside.

- Jesus got baptised to show everyone he was going to take their sin away.

- Jesus heard a voice from God saying how much God loved him and saw the Holy Spirit come upon him.

Ask which miracle Jesus had done before this point in his life? (It's a trick question – he hadn't done one yet.) Ask which sermon or story Jesus had told before this point in his life? (Again, a trick question – he hadn't told one yet.)

So God said to him, 'This is my Son, whom I love; with him I am well pleased' even though Jesus hadn't done anything!!

We always assume that people will only love us or like us if we *do* something to deserve it. But the Bible tells us that we are special in God's eyes because we are who we are, not because of anything we may have done. It's an amazing fact, because it goes against everything we think.

Keep repeating the phrase 'God loves us because we are who we are, not because of anything we may have done.' You may want to say a few things that you have achieved in life and say after each one: 'But I know that God loves me because of who I am not because I did ...'

Say that in your service you have baptised *[Name]* and in doing so have reminded all of us that we are special in God's eyes. Today *[Name]* and their family and friends have been reminded that God loves *[Name]* and died so that *[Name]* could be washed on the inside – but you have also been reminded that *[Name]*, their family, friends and every single one of you is very, very special in God's eyes.

Statement of what we believe

These are included in the Baptism Liturgy, but you may like to have a brief time of additional intercessions, praying that people might know that they are special in God's eyes, especially those who are:

- Lonely because of their work or family situation.
- Being bullied at school or work.
- Live in places where there is war or hatred.
- Ill in any way or who have lost someone in their family.

Ending

Ask if everyone feels they are special as a result of your time together and say that you would like to hear the answer to the question 'Are you special?' with an enthusiastic and convincing 'I'm special!' You may need to do this several times! Conclude with a prayer thanking God that all of us are special in his eyes and asking that everyone may live their lives in the coming days in such a way as to know that love.

You are special!

No, you really <u>ARE</u> special!

Yes, this means you . . .
. . . you are special!

Not the person sitting
next to you . . .
I mean you . . .

. . . you are special!

You are incredibly,
utterly, absolutely and
totally . . .

. . . SPECIAL!

Hang on...

...I am am special!

Jesus' baptism

'This is my Son, whom I love; with him I am well pleased.'
(Matthew 6:17)

- People got baptised by John as a sign that they wanted to be clean on the inside

- John didn't want to baptise Jesus, because he knew he was already clean on the inside

- Jesus got baptised to show everyone he was going to take away their sin.

- Jesus heard a voice from God saying how much God loved him and saw the Holy Spirit come upon him.